Curated Moments

Reggio-Inspired Classrooms for Infants, Toddlers, and Twos

Jennifer Kesselring, MEd • Whitney Dickinson
Ashley Stewart • Jerry Bates, MEd

www.gryphonhouse.com

Copyright

Published by Gryphon House, Inc.
P. O. Box 10, Lewisville, NC 27023

800.638.0928; 877.638.7576 [fax]

Visit us on the web at www.gryphonhouse.com.

Cover image courtesy of the authors. Interior images courtesy of the authors.

Library of Congress Control Number: 2024932355

Bulk Purchase

Gryphon House books are available for special premiums and sales promotions as well as for fund-raising use. Special editions or book excerpts also can be created to specifications. For details, call 800.638.0928.

Disclaimer

Gryphon House, Inc., cannot be held responsible for damage, mishap, or injury incurred during the use of or because of activities in this book. Appropriate and reasonable caution and adult supervision of children involved in activities and corresponding to the age and capability of each child involved are recommended at all times. Do not leave children unattended at any time. Observe safety and caution at all times.

This book is not intended to give legal or financial advice. All financial and legal opinions contained herein are from the personal research and experience of the author and are intended as educational material. Seek the advice of a qualified legal advisor or financial advisor before making legal or financial decisions.

Dedication

This book is dedicated to all the educators and visionaries who have contributed to the ongoing evolution and innovation at Riverfield. We express our gratitude for your unwavering commitment to the highest quality learning experiences for young children.

Table of Contents

Foreword

Dear Readers:

Welcome to your participation in this book, which has developed from many enjoyable moments that have taken place at Riverfield Country Day School in Tulsa, Oklahoma. The projects, experiences, explorations, experiments, and values are inspired by the Reggio approach, from Reggio Emilia, Italy. I am Amelia Gambetti, and I started to collaborate with Riverfield Country Day School in 2008, before the exhibit "The Wonder of Learning—The Hundred Languages of Children" went to Tulsa. I am referring to a dialogue between two different educational experiences that have different origins, different contexts, different cultures, a different history, and that are located on different continents. They have, though, something really important in common: they share the same commitment to invest in early childhood and in enhancing the value of education and its quality. Has this dialogue perhaps created another educational experience? Could this commitment, this investment in education, offer a contribution to a better present and future society? Personally, I think so.

Nice meeting you all, dear readers, who have chosen to read this book because you believe in the importance of an education that has the aim to "start strong" from an early age, when children, full of potentialities, have many interests and curiosities. Children ask the adults to listen to and participate with them in the construction of learning processes, but then, are children always listened to?

When I visited Riverfield for the first time, I walked the classrooms of children from a few months to five years old, and although children were not present, I could definitely feel that they were there because I could "hear" their voices, and I could picture them in the different areas full of engaging, attractive provocations, materials, techniques, and media. I felt I could participate in the life of the school with them, their educators, and their families. Even though only two administrators took me around, I had the impression I was surrounded by a complex educational context full of life, pleasure, experiences, challenges, and excitement, and most of all, full of the joy of learning made visible through documentation panels telling the stories of many activities and projects.

My collaboration with Riverfield has continued to the present day. I would like to share with you that when I sometimes hear educators elsewhere saying it is more difficult to be with young children because they do not talk, I am perplexed and even a little sad. While they don't speak with words, even very young children talk and communicate in many ways.

This book offers evidence of many young children's deep dialogues with their peers, with the adults, with the environment, with materials, and through the "hundred languages of children." Very young children like talking; they like to express themselves. My question is whether the adults available are able to hear what they say. Are the adults paying attention to what they do? Are they paying attention to their expressions, their gestures, their movements, the ways in which they build relationships? Do the adults have the capability to interpret children's "languages" that don't necessarily have words as a component?

This book gives visibility to a strong image of the child, of the school, and of the educators who, through theory and practice intertwined and through professional development and research, are part of complex explorations, full of analysis and reflections. The educators are seen as builders of attitudes based on listening, observing, interpreting, and documenting in partnership with children. Cameras and other technology are tools in the hands of children and adults who have the goal to capture details of different experiences and aim to give evidence to the way in which knowledge is built, through the value of collaboration and the value of different perspectives.

Loris Malaguzzi, the founder of the Reggio approach, used to say, "Nothing without joy," a joy that asks to be interpreted also as an effort in succeeding complex and meaningful results through challenges, problem solving, and creative and cognitive processes of learning. This applies to children, educators, and parents.

Throughout this book, we see educators who have an image of a child who has rights instead of needs, a child who has been competent since birth, a child full of potentialities, resources, and capabilities, and a child who has the right to learn with joy. I think that this is a wonderful and thoughtful disposition for all adults, as it lends hope and space for looking at children from a new point of view. I invite all of you as readers to also include in your thinking and in your vision a stronger image of a competent child who never stops amazing us.

With affection, my best wishes for your life,

Amelia Gambetti

Educator, Former Reggio Emilia Liaison, and Consultant of the Reggio Approach

Preface

"Nothing without joy."
—Loris Malaguzzi

What does it mean to us to be inspired by the Reggio approach? Rooted in progressive ideas and always evolving, Riverfield has remained committed to the highest quality learning for children since its inception in 1984. Thus, it was no surprise when an encounter with the Reggio approach through the "Hundred Languages of Children" exhibit in Oklahoma City was both fascinating and enticing. The Reggio approach, founded in Reggio Emilia, Italy, by Loris Malaguzzi, has been touted as the world's best example of the highest quality early childhood learning environments in the world. Although Riverfield and the municipal infant-toddler centers and preschools of Reggio Emilia are each born and steeped in their own strong and unique stories and identities, both contexts are committed to high-quality education and to viewing school as an ongoing place of research.

Many avenues have supported the ongoing conversation between Riverfield and the Reggio Children organization over twenty-five years. We have read and "unpacked" the many publications of Reggio Children. We have attended presentations at the conferences of the National Association for the Education of Young Children (NAEYC) and the North American Reggio Emilia Alliance. We have participated in study groups in Reggio Emilia and started a collaboration and consultancy with Amelia Gambetti, a former educator in Reggio Emilia. We serve on boards and committees that share the inspiration from the educational experience in Reggio Emilia.

For more on the Reggio approach, visit the Reggio Children website at https://www.reggiochildren.it/en/

One of the most powerful sources of exchange and understanding came from supporting the "Wonder of Learning: The Hundred Languages of Children" exhibit in our community. Housed in Tulsa for six months, the exhibit and its many panel discussions shared the foundational values of the educational philosophy and told the story of how it has changed and evolved and how the philosophy and commitment to quality came to life through the joyful actions and thinking of children, educators, and families. This exhibit became a powerful tool for reflection and advocacy for quality in education within our school, our community, and the many out-of-state learning communities that traveled to see and study it. It also served as a strong reminder that with great effort comes great joy.

It is important to note that the experience of the infant-toddler centers and preschools in Reggio Emilia is not one that can be copied or adopted. It is, instead, a philosophy, a unique experience, a way of being in and thinking about school, children, and adults learning together. It is an educational experience born in the context of Reggio Emilia and its history. We think that it demands that each individual and program take into consideration their own identities, experiences, and beliefs and then gain inspiration for deepening their commitment and work through the educational principles of the Reggio approach. Again, these principles are not a recipe or a boxed curriculum but are a compass that helps orient thinking, weaving theory and practice together.

We remain committed to advocacy for this way of thinking about and living education. As we heard in our study group in Reggio Emilia in March 2023, "Education remains the first line of defense in a tumultuous world."

Resources on Reggio Emilia

Ceppi, Giulio, and Michele Zini, eds. 1998. *Children, Spaces, Relations: Metaproject for an Environment for Young Children*. Reggio Emilia, IT: Reggio Children.

Edwards, Carolyn, Lella Gandini, and George Forman, eds. 2011. *The Hundred Languages of Children: The Reggio Emilia Experience in Transformation*. 3rd ed. Westport, CT: Praeger.

Malaguzzi, Loris, and Paola Cagliari. 2018. *Brick by Brick: History of the XXV April People's Nursery School of Villa Cella*. Reggio Emilia, IT: Reggio Children.

Municipality of Reggio Emilia. 2010. *Indications: Preschools and Infant-Toddler Centres of the Municipality of Reggio Emilia*. English ed. Reggio Emilia, IT: Reggio Children.

Reggio Children. 2011. *The Wonder of Learning*. Reggio Emilia, IT: Reggio Children.

Rinaldi, Carlina. 2006. *In Dialogue with Reggio Emilia: Listening, Researching, and Learning*. London, UK: Routledge.

Vecchi, Vea. 2010. *Art and Creativity in Reggio Emilia: Exploring the Role and Potential of Ateliers in Early Childhood Education*. London, UK: Routledge.

Introduction

Through interpretations at Riverfield Country Day School, an independent school in Tulsa, Oklahoma, this book makes visible the premise that environments and the experiences within them have the potential to serve as catalysts for multifaceted play and learning. Positioned within infant and toddler classrooms, the stories of rich inquiry, robust environments, intelligent materials, and complex experiences accentuate the many creative, cognitive, and joyful discoveries of very young children. Inspired by the experiences of the infant-toddler centers and preschools in Reggio Emilia, Italy, the authors encourage educators to reimagine school as a place of research. Imagine school as a place where environments and the materials that fill the shelves are curated to create innovative occasions for exploration and learning. Readers will find pages filled with photographic essays and narration of children and teachers from two infant classrooms, three one-to-two-year-old classrooms, and three two-to-three-year-old classrooms. The children are immersed in interesting scenarios that emphasize the ongoing reciprocal relationships between theory and practice, inquiry and learning, observation, analysis, and action, and joy and work.

How This Book Is Organized

In the first section, we focus on research in action, introducing readers to curated macro- and microenvironments found throughout Riverfield's preschool. We unpack the permeating philosophy, mindsets, dispositions, thinking, and systems that inform and inspire action. We examine how these perspectives translate into ways in which creative, cognitive, and joyful experiences support children in uncovering big ideas. Readers will encounter Riverfield's interpretation of a cycle of inquiry, a knowledge-building process that intertwines observation, documentation, analysis, design, curation, and action to deepen the children's unfolding action research. In this cycle of inquiry, theory and practice walk hand in hand as educators and children explore the role the environment, materials, and curated experiences have in learning scenarios. In this way of thinking and learning, the cycle is continuous, as one inquiry leads to the uncovering of the next big idea.

Readers can delve into the thinking and process of designing and creating environments and installations that are intentional and responsive to children's curiosities, development, and the social nature of learning.

The second section of the book represents a visual odyssey, a diary of experiences within eight infant and toddler classrooms. Through photography, teacher narratives, and reflections, readers are invited into the thinking, processes, and analysis of curated microenvironments and occasions for discovery. The snapshots are windows into the realm of intelligence, curiosity, experimentation, discovery, and the social construction of knowledge. These moments encapsulate the natural fascination, boundless creativity, and unbridled joy that unfold when young children navigate inviting and complex environments with agency and confidence.

Instead of focusing on the series of occasions that thread themselves through one year in one classroom, we organized the book in a way that shares a variety of experiences from several classrooms over a few years. We have included experiences from two infant classrooms, three toddler classrooms, and three two-year-old classrooms. This was a hard choice because we value threads of continuity in which one occasion for learning, when observed, documented, and analyzed, informs the design and curation of the next and holds us accountable to walking closely alongside the children and their interests. But, we weighed this against the potential for readers to encounter a wider variety of environments, materials, and experiences, as well as the thinking behind them, and we chose the latter. We kindly ask that you stay close to the understanding that none of the experiences in this book happened in isolation or without informed intention. All of the stories we share are rooted in observation and analysis of the children's interests, strategies, curiosities, and cognitive knots over many threaded concepts and experiences. We do our best to situate each story within a short context of previous encounters and thinking, but the main idea is that as educators we offer a world full of curious possibilities to children.

We would be remiss if we didn't mention that our choice of materials and the ways in which we curate experiences might challenge some readers. We are not an ordinary school with a standard outlook on infant and toddler education. That may be uncomfortable for some. You may question some materials, and we welcome that. We have found, however, that if we hold space for "we could if" thinking, we open possibilities for children that are far richer than those we offer if our initial reaction stops at "we can't because." So, we ask that you try on "what if" as you browse the pages of this book. Perhaps you will discover new ways of seeing, thinking, or acting to bump against what you have held as certain.

Incorporating Technology

It is important to note that one of our strong intentions for the past decade has been innovative strategies for embracing the digital world. This action research project, which we have named Echoes of Reality, seeks to build understanding regarding the many ways that the tangible and intangible worlds can combine to create layered realities. We remain committed to choosing and using technology with the same philosophy and values with which we choose all materials. We are constantly asking ourselves how these tools invite complex thinking and development of the cognitive and creative intelligences. We have found, for instance, that digital microscopes offer a unique opportunity to examine the world with both micro- and macroperspectives: Digital projections of various landscapes invite children into an augmented experience of reality. Mirrored boxes extend this augmented reality in interesting ways.

We have found that the most effective integration of technology occurs when teachers stay closely attached to the "we can if" research attitude and remain committed to navigating the ambiguity, risk, and open-ended possibility associated with learning something new. Thus, as the need or desire to integrate a new technology emerges, teachers embrace the mindset of learning through doing. Although we set aside time to "mess about" with new materials, the bulk of the learning occurs alongside children, who tend to be adept and natural in their relationships with technology. As teachers experiment with various materials, they undergo a parallel learning process, discovering innovative ways to present concepts, facilitate learning, and adapt to the diverse needs of their students while developing their own skillsets with the particular tool. This active involvement creates an important empathy for the learning children do. Involvement not only enhances teachers' pedagogical understandings but also instills a sense of resilience, adaptability, and stronger fluency. Teachers evolve as colearners with children, taking risks and weaving their newfound insights into the daily experiences with children. Simultaneously, children witness the transformative power of lifelong learning supported by curiosity, experimentation, resilience, and invention. If a technology tool is not readily available in the school, the teacher can rely on the spirit of collaboration with the broader community. Establishing connections with community resources, such as local artisans, scientists, or craftspeople, enriches the learning experience for both teachers and students.

Equipped with advanced tools and technology, fab labs (fabrication laboratories) and makerspaces are havens for creativity and innovation. These spaces give teachers access to a plethora of materials, from 3-D printers to laser cutters. We have found many community resources eager to collaborate with us and allow us to use technological tools and to offer us hands-on experiences and training. We have found some valuable local resources that you may have in your area as well:

- **Fab labs:** Search for your local fab lab to set up times for messing about and for classes to learn the logistics of the different technologies.
- **Libraries:** Research local libraries to find makerspaces that offer use of 3-D printers, vinyl cutters, small laser cutters, and recording studios, as well as classes to deepen your understanding of how to integrate these tools.
- **Educational institutions:** Make connections with local schools, colleges, and universities, and share or borrow resources or ideas.
- **Children's museums:** Build a relationship with your local children's museum to develop your understanding of curated installations, innovative thinking, and hands-on experiences for children.

- **Network of like-minded colleagues:** Seek others who hold similar values around education and the integration of technology.
- **Pottery studios:** Local pottery studios and clay producers are great resources for purchasing clay and glaze and for firing clay artifacts that the children create.
- **Parks and recreation:** Your local department may offer specialized classes and equipment.
- **Photographers:** Professionals, studios, or family members with photography backgrounds may offer photography courses or online tutorials. Professional development can help teachers understand how to document and analyze children's learning.
- **Public school districts:** Some will sell used science equipment, such as digital microscopes.
- **Online retailers:** We have found shopping for rope lights, spotlights, and other specialty lighting is best after the holiday season when prices are discounted. We have also ordered a variety of small digital microscopes through online retailers at a minimal cost.

A Word about Budgets

Please know that there is often a misunderstanding regarding independent schools and budgets. We function on a tight budget in the same way that so many early learning contexts must. We have made intentional choices for our spending to reflect our values and philosophy. For example, instead of purchasing plastic counting bears, we use reclaimed and recycled materials such as corks or stones. Our shelves are lined with open-ended materials, or loose parts, that are donated by local businesses and families. Our teachers collect and sanitize take-out containers and gather recycled jars and plastic containers to organize and display materials. The children bring collections from family members' sewing rooms or garages for textile areas or makerspaces. These strategies, apart from contributing to a smaller carbon footprint, let us use funds to purchase technology and high-grade art materials while still honoring the budgetary constraints of our school.

- **Family connections:** Talk with families in your class or school community to learn about their hobbies and knowledge bases and how they might share those with your school.
- **Sewing shops:** Local sewing shops often host classes that teach the basics of sewing and can offer ideas for textile studios.
- **Plastic supply companies:** This is, hands down, one of the most used resources in our community. We have been able to get acrylic scraps and other interesting materials for construction areas.

- **Families:** Each year, our educators send letters to the families with a list of possibilities for open-ended materials. As families clean out drawers and closets, they send their donations to repurpose and use in the school. Keeping families informed on projects and installation ideas helps them better understand the materials we are seeking and repurposing for projects.
- **Local arts and humanities councils:** They often have resources for connecting with local artisans, performers, ballet companies, theater groups, symphonies, and so on.
- **Flower shops:** We have several agreements with local florists to collect flowers that are beginning to wilt or fade. We simply collect them at the end of every week.
- **Hardware stores:** Ask local hardware stores about their scrap bins, and take time to search through the pieces for materials to develop your makerspaces.

It is our hope that, as readers encounter the many occasions narrated through this book, they will uncover the pedagogical choices of the educators, the dynamic interplay between the environment and the children, the ongoing conversations between the children and materials, and the interplay among open-ended experiences and children's creative and cognitive intelligences. We believe that if children are immersed in this environment, they can experience education as a grand adventure of inquiry, experimentation, action, and social construction of knowledge. And if that is what education is, then we can inspire a lifelong love of the learning process. What better gift could we offer young children than that?

Section I:

School as a Place of Research

Chapter 1: Research in Action

> *"Education is not preparation for life; education is life itself."*
>
> —John Dewey,
> philosopher, psychologist, and education reformer

As I turn the corner of the infant-toddler hallway into a color lab, I am greeted by a large, white floor canvas that is alive with materials in various shades of blues, greens, and purples and overlaid with a projection of a peacock. This sensory experience is further enriched by the recorded sounds of one of our resident peacocks, along with his feathers, numerous textural elements, and reflective surfaces of various shapes and sizes. The invitation is one of many in this space that focuses on the ways in which color plays with light, reflection, and everyday experiences on our campus. Having watched the peacock outside their window strut his emerging feathers for several days, the teachers have thoughtfully translated this encounter into an immersive sensorial palette. Five young children sit near each other: Three are playing with white tulle that has seemingly captured the peacock within it. Another is grasping a peacock feather, and yet another is enchanted with a blue cupcake liner that echoes the familiar hues of a peacock. The teacher is nearby taking notes and photographs while carefully listening to and observing the nuances of the children's interactions—watching for curling toes, reaching out a finger or hand, the gaze of an eye, the "thinking tongue," or joyful coos that indicate the myriad ways thinking and learning are flourishing.

At Riverfield Country Day School in Tulsa, Oklahoma, these kinds of invitations are at the heart of our everyday lives. Steeped in social constructivism—a philosophy that believes children construct their knowledge through conversation and interaction with each other, with teachers, with the environment, and with materials. We embrace school as a working laboratory, a place of research, where hands and minds work in unison and the creative and cognitive are always in tandem. It is a place where environments, materials, inquiry, and interesting invitations beckon learning that remains alive.

John Dewey, an educational philosopher and reformer, famously proclaimed, "Education is not preparation for life. Education is life itself," and we have found this to be both compelling and accurate as we work alongside children in their innate quest for knowledge. Carlina Rinaldi, President of Reggio Children Foundation, unpacks John Dewey's quote in the following profound way in *The Hundred Languages of Children* (Edwards, Gandini, and Forman, 2011):

> When we say that school is not a preparation for life but is life, this means assuming the responsibility to create a context in which words such as *creativity, change, innovation, error, doubt*, and *uncertainty*, when used on a daily basis, can truly be developed and become real. This means creating a context in which the teaching-learning relationship is highly evolved. That is, where the solution to certain problems leads to the emergence of new questions, new expectations, and new changes. This also means creating a context in which children, from a very young age, discover that there are problems that are not easily resolved, that perhaps cannot have an answer. For this reason, they are the most wonderful problems because therein lies the spirit of research.

At Riverfield, we use the inquiry cycle as a way to orient our thinking and strategy toward this "spirit of research." Believing that learning begins with really good questions and then follows a continuous cycle of inquiry and reflection, teachers set up robust environments full of intelligent materials and curate occasions that pique curiosity and adventure. Throughout the encounters, children are engaged in action research as they grapple with interesting concepts, experiment with action and reaction, uncover big ideas, discover connections, apply knowledge from previous experiences, and build relationships—cognitively, creatively, emotionally, and socially. Working and playing alongside the children, teachers carefully observe, document, and analyze the encounters of the individuals and the group to understand more fully the children's strategies; what ideas or concepts they are wrestling with; how they approach the environment, materials, and experiences; and how they build meaning and knowledge individually and as a group. Based on the actions and reactions of the children, teachers self-reflect by actively questioning and critiquing their choice of materials, group composition, how and when they lent knowledge or nudges, and the timing

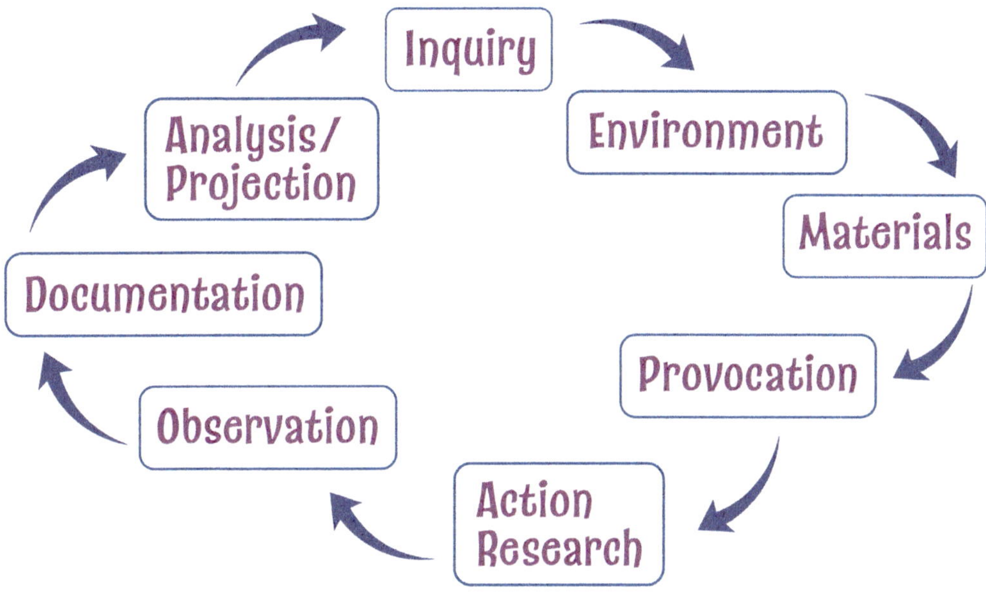

and nature of the questions they asked. They also seek the perspectives of colleagues, and at times, family members, to find ways to refine the experience, add complexity, deepen the play, thinking, and learning, and represent all of it through their documentation. Drawing from their conclusions, teachers brainstorm and design possibilities for the next query and provocative occasion. In this way, research becomes woven into the fabric of daily life. Children begin to rely on the solidarity between their role as active protagonists and the role of their teacher as a provocateur of questions and on the process of constructing answers. As Carlina Rinaldi states in *The Hundred Languages of Children* (Edwards, Gandini, and Forman, 2011), "Children appreciate the fact that we are right there by their side in the search for their answers: the child-researcher and the teacher-researcher."

But what does "research" look like in the life of a young child or for the teachers who work with them? Creating a culture in which school is an ongoing place of research is complex and fascinating. It implies that everyone is seeking that which they do not know. It provokes courageous learning and adventure. It means that everyone spends their days immersed in curiosity and thinking, that beautiful questions abound, that the environment is robust enough to support inquisition through experience. It means that the intelligent materials lend the affordance of learning through doing. It means that active listening becomes part of the pedagogy, that the role of the child and the role of the teacher shift in interesting ways as they become partners in learning processes. It means that theory and practice have a reciprocal relationship, where one informs the other in an ongoing way.

The Role of Curiosity and Wonder

Teachers recognize that children do not wait for our permission to think. They encourage the ongoing construction, deconstruction, and reconstruction of meaning and knowledge. In this type of school, the child is no longer seen as weak and passive, nor as a vessel to be filled, but instead as a strong protagonist and an active contributor to their own experience and learning. Because, as a school, we embrace that children construct knowledge socially, through posing questions, acting on their curiosity, and manipulating their environment alongside their peers, we curate a culture where research is designed to be social, alive, interesting, and full of action and possibilities. It is a place where children are immersed in questions, multiple perspectives, disequilibrium, cognitive dissonance, and open-ended processes through which they take risks to build collaborative answers. To create scenarios that meet the students' agency and interest, the teacher must also remain inquisitive and masters of their craft—designing, watching, and listening carefully, and making attempts to responsively alter the environment or materials within it. With careful observation and supported by documentation and thoughtful interpretation, teachers can confidently design rich and meaningful experiences where—with peers' help and the teachers' scaffolding—learning is inevitable. Through this process, the students and teachers become a community of intrinsically motivated learners who cultivate their curiosity and sense of wonder.

> "The illiterate of the 21st century will not be those who cannot read and write, but those who cannot learn, unlearn, and relearn."
>
> —ALVIN TOFFLER
> FUTURIST AND AUTHOR

The Image of the Environment

The Municipality of Reggio Emilia, Italy, produced a booklet, *Indications: Preschools and Infant-Toddler Centres of the Municipality of Reggio Emilia*, a concise description of the identity, aims, principles, and the essential elements for the operations of infant-toddler centers in Reggio Emilia. In the English edition, the booklet shares, "The environment interacts with, is modified by, and takes shape in relation to the projects and learning experiences of the children and of the adults in a constant dialogue between architecture and pedagogy."

If the teacher, as an active and dynamic protagonist, walks alongside the children as strong and competent learners, what role does the environment play in a school acting as a place of research? If the environment is designed to be an additional teacher, then it provides intentional, collaborative, rich, and complex spaces that invite children to become questioners, designers, experimenters, inventors, deconstructors, builders, and negotiators of theories. A robust environment means a context and condition that is full of possibilities.

It is a place where, by design, the learner can meet and encounter big ideas and concepts, a space that poses questions, creates cognitive knots, and invites the cognitive and creative intelligences to evolve side by side.

Inherent in the environment are spaces that offer opportunity for small groups to work together; spaces for both independent and facilitated experiences; spaces that invite conversation, exchange, negotiation, and problem solving; and spaces that allow for children's work to be iterative, with many edits and renditions, and span over several days or weeks. The many spaces in a room become an ecosystem of their own, with a strong identity full of fascinating materials, and by their curation and organization alone, invite interesting encounters.

When designing environments with this goal in mind, the traditional elements of a preschool classroom take on new life. The dramatic play area transforms into a miniature version of home with light fixtures hanging from the ceiling, cupboards stocked with beautiful plates and interesting pots and pans, attractive dress-up clothes hanging in a wardrobe, a palette of empty make-up containers and brushes laid out on a small dressing table, and open-ended materials that beckon storytelling and imaginative play. Likewise, in addition to unit blocks, a construction area provides lengths of cove molding or cardboard tubes set next to small balls to invite experimentation with the physics of incline and motion. Additionally, doorknobs, carabiner clips, strands of rope, pulleys, small tiles, PVC pipes in various sizes, measuring tapes, drafting supplies, seashells, sea glass, and dominoes afford building with architectural detail in mind.

It is also a space where digital landscapes offer floor-to-ceiling projections that augment experiences as backdrops to the construction. A video of a roller coaster might play on a backdrop shadow screen as the children play with incline and motion. Or a picture of downtown might be projected as children build with white materials and add digital drawings on top of their structures.

Tinkering and maker spaces beckon children to innovation and invention with chipboard, fasteners, tape, wood, drills, screwdrivers, clamps, rubber bands, bottle caps, small wheels, straws, stirring sticks, and a plethora of other interesting objects. One of our favorite memories from a tinkering space in a toddler classroom is when we ordered new shelves and included the children, with their safety goggles and electric screwdrivers, in the construction of the shelves. They were remarkably competent at the task and ever so proud to have contributed in such an important way. A week later, however, we became acutely aware that when toddlers learn how to put shelves together with power tools, they have also learned how to take them apart. This too, was a moment of great pride for the children and a moment of insightful and poignant laughter for us. But now we know. Among the many other shared agreements we make with children regarding the tools and materials of the classroom, leaving furniture put together is now part of our agreements.

In an attempt to blur the boundaries between the indoors and outdoors, we invite the wonders of nature to become an integral part of our learning experiences in spaces dedicated to natural materials. Full of seeds, pods, pinecones, and other materials gathered by the children on their walks to the woods; dried flowers donated by families; and mortars and pestles for grinding, bowls for mixing, and scoops for stirring, this space entices the children to create, explore, and collaborate. Intentionally designed in an area of the classroom with floor-to-ceiling windows, the natural atelier invites the children to regularly reference the outdoors when working. In this way, changes in seasons, shifts in weather, and nuances of campus wildlife remain constant resources for children's thinking and action. It is common to see the peacocks strutting in front of the windows or the deer prancing across the football field, offering limitless inspiration to the children.

A collection of complex spaces such as those listed, and any others that are designed from year to year in response to interests and motivations of the children and teachers, help create a robust environment where learning is dynamic, social, and active. Understanding that life is complex and not isolated into "domains," we hold children and ourselves highly capable and believe that children deserve the rich nature of an integrated world. Thus, teachers remain committed to offering such environments to children as an integral component of deep learning, engaged living, and empowering children to embrace and navigate the many complexities of life.

The Image of Intelligent Materials

For a robust environment to reach its full potential, it must contain a large amount and variety of materials with intelligent potential. What do we mean when we talk about *intelligent materials*? At our school, intelligent materials are those that promote high levels of thinking and, as we have heard educators in Reggio Emilia say and as author Mara Krechevsky synthesizes: "Intelligent materials are those that charm, trick, and amuse children. They provoke, stimulate, engage, connect, and can evoke imagination and emotion. The materials do not impose a prescribed direction but pose questions, elicit hypotheses, test theories, and challenge children to experiment, design, and create" (Giudici, Rinaldi, and Krechevsky, 2001). Intelligent materials are made of a variety of textures, forms, subtle and well-chosen colors, sizes, compositions, reflective properties, and manipulability. They invite questions, curiosity, and experimentation, involve a balance of simplicity and complexity, and facilitate the creation of stories, metaphors, and games. Perhaps most importantly, intelligent materials lead to a sense of wonder and excitement so that children are motivated to engage with them again and again—discovering more with each interaction.

"Children have endless capabilities for building relationships with complex contexts, with other children and adults, with the community, with environments, and with many materials."

—Amelia Gambetti

To highlight the power of intelligent materials, one example we often use is a pink plastic piece of cake. If, in your dramatic play area, children encounter a pink piece of cake, it will be a piece of cake every time and in every situation. It is prescribed in nature. If, however, the children encounter a basket of ribbons or bottle caps in dramatic play, these materials have the potential to be something different or serve a unique purpose every time. These things require imagination and often negotiation among friends to determine their role in that moment. So, by their open-ended nature, they demand a different vigor in thinking, communicating, and playing. The materials themselves seem to entice experiences and communicate to children that they are competent.

We have heard educators in Reggio Emilia refer to the "hundred languages of children" when speaking of the ways in which children can use materials to construct and express their thinking. They talk about giving equal dignity to both verbal and nonverbal languages, and as Amelia Gambetti so eloquently stated in one of our weekly conversations:

> The concept is related to a communication strategy that has the desire, the interest, and the curiosity to include cognitive and creative aspects, based on different ways to express ourselves beyond the verbal language. Therefore, media, techniques, and a wide range of materials offer to us new development of our intelligences. In addition, they offer a possibility to articulate our verbal language using far more detail that can be borrowed from the expressivity that other materials lend. In this way, we encounter richer contexts for the well-being of our mind and soul.

Thus, when designing an environment, we consider the many ways materials can summon children to make visible their unfolding discoveries and theories or to express the imaginations and emotions the materials may evoke. For example, an art shelf can morph into an art studio by increasing the quality, complexity, and inherent potential of the materials offered. In addition to crayons and markers, shelves can be filled with artist-grade materials, such as oil and chalk pastels, sketching pencils, watercolor pencils, markers in all hues and shades of color, clay and clay tools, watercolor paints, brushes, and paper. Sewing notions and small sewing machines, an array of small treasures for collage, weaving looms and a collection of materials for weaving, paper of all sizes, weights and textures, and natural materials invite exploration.

The materials are conduits for choice, inquiry, thinking, creativity, and innovation, and provide children agency, engagement, and self-efficacy. They invite the children's creative and cognitive intelligences to develop side by side as they manipulate, transform, design, and create. In short, intelligent materials lend themselves as a tool for constructing mindsets, dispositions, and knowledge through creatively and joyfully questioning and doing—again, reinforcing that learning is dynamic and is an active rather than passive process.

The Image of the Teacher

In traditional schooling, the teacher's role is often as the one who imparts knowledge. In many preschools, the teacher is relegated to that of a basic caregiver. As a school, we know that care must be pervasive and is very important, as is lending knowledge or strategy when the timing and the approach are intentionally considered. In a school steeped in research, the teacher moves beyond that of expert or caregiver and is empowered as a strong agent for designing cultures and experiences full of questioning and thinking. Instead of imparting knowledge, the teacher creates an environment conducive to actively constructing knowledge and has the responsibility to nudge the child's thinking by asking the right questions at the right time and for the right reasons.

One strategy teachers employ to pose questions in an interesting way is by intentionally designing robust environments full of intelligent materials and curating rich experiences that invite exploration, cognitive knots, risk, problem solving, and fun. To keep these environments and experiences dynamic and responsive, and to ensure that the construction and negotiation of answers is a collective and ongoing pursuit, educators must be nuanced moderators of conversation and thoughtful documenters and analysts. After curating and offering an environment or experience to children, they must carefully watch and record children's reactions, strategies, conversations (verbal and nonverbal), subtleties, gestures, microgestures, facial expressions, and actions. Based on these observations, teachers then hypothesize new directions and formulate experiences that naturally build on and extend previous encounters. In this way, teachers perpetually challenge children's current understanding and provoke growth and development in their thinking and action. This kind of documentation serves as visible listening and may include teacher observations and reflections, conversations with children, photographic images, videos, and artifacts the children have created. Through this process, the teacher makes visible the learning, the strategies, and the theories of both the individual and of the group as they highlight the competencies, learning, and joy of the children.

> "The teacher's role centers on provoking occasions of discovery through a kind of alert, inspired listening and stimulation of children's dialogue, co-action, and co-construction of knowledge."
>
> —*The Hundred Languages of Children* (2011)

In addition to observing and documenting, teachers should take time to reflect on and analyze the documentation with the children, themselves, and other colleagues. It is through this reflective process that children remember, articulate, and synthesize their experiences. Teachers also gain insight and a better understanding of the ways in which the children

> "From the very beginning, curiosity and learning refute that which is simple and isolated. Children yearn to discover the measures and relations of complex situations."
>
> —LORIS MALAGUZZI, FOUNDER OF THE REGGIO EMILIA APPROACH

perceived the experience, the ways they as educators set up an encounter, and formed groups, and how the materials they chose and curated influenced the learning and joy of the invitation. Sharing work with colleagues and subsequent shared analysis also allows for multiple perspectives, adding to the understanding, complexity, and intentionality of learning experiences. This empowers teachers to continually design for learning that is relevant and contextualized, walks alongside the curiosities of the children, and encourages children to create connections, relationships, and meaning within their world. It also affords the opportunity to model productive collaboration for students, which immerses them in a culture of collaboration and reciprocal exchange.

The Role of Integrated Experiences

We believe that learning should be fun, full of engagement, and sparked by curiosity. Therefore, while a quality experience for children should integrate the domains of knowledge, it should also invite adventure and social encounters and should honor the pleasures of childhood. The synthesis of questions, materials, and environments manifests in thoughtful and alluring experiences. These experiences are not isolated but grounded in observation and documentation of children's interests and experiences, as well as the beliefs about how children learn. The end result is an occasion, or multiple occasions, that invite children in through all of their senses, engage their minds and bodies, demand effort, and bring great joy. Throughout this book, we explore this process and multiple integrated experiences from Riverfield Country Day School that include complex environments, intelligent materials, and active learning for all.

Creating a culture in which school is an ongoing place of research is complex and fascinating. It battles against banality, mediocrity, and boredom. It provokes courageous learning and adventure. It relies on an image of highly capable children, teachers, environments, materials, and integrated experiences. It also empowers children and teachers to become a community of intrinsically motivated learners who continuously cultivate their curiosity and sense of wonder. Inherent in the design of the working laboratory are robust environments filled with intelligent materials that, through their curation and organization, create interesting experiences and beckon learning that remains alive. In this kind of environment, supported by the cycle of inquiry, children and teachers rely on the solidarity between their role as active protagonists, the role of the teacher and the environment as a provocateur of questions, and on the social process of constructing answers.

It's Just

Chapter 2: Curating Environments and Microenvironments

"I have a really great idea I'd like to pursue. Could we set up a time to talk?" As a leader in education, these are exciting words to hear from a teacher, words ripe with potential and inviting invention. As educators, we have the extraordinary privilege and responsibility to curate environments that kindle the flames of exploration, learning, and creativity. Note that curating an environment is much more than arranging furniture and placing toys. It is designing a complex space that is responsive to the needs and interests of its inhabitants, inspires inquiry and ignites adventure, honors the role of aesthetics and beauty in the learning process, beckons social encounters in the construction of knowledge, is responsive and dynamic, and makes play and learning inevitable. Curating and organizing a collection of interesting, intelligent, and open-ended materials and displaying them in a way that is both beautiful and "readable" to children offers the materials' potential and how they might be used. Curation implies an act of love and is an investment in the children and in our professional growth. It serves as an affirmation of the commitment to being open to possibilities. "We can if . . ." is a motto in the process, a mantra reminding us to remain responsive to the children's interests, lean into the unknown and the dissonance it can create, and stay unwavering in our dedication to the idea that anything is possible.

The Importance of Complexity

What does it mean when we say *complex*? A complex environment is one that has layers of possibility embedded in the materials, organization, systems, and potential encounters. It is a space where the shelves are filled with well-organized and multifaceted tools with which children can experiment, construct, create, imagine, and invent. When a space offers complexity, it fully supports small-group as well as individual work and play. Complexity also affords children's finding and solving problems together. It is antithetical to "sad and lonely." When creating a microenvironment dedicated to the care of baby dolls, one would not have a single doll, devoid of clothes and without accessories. Instead, an area would be designed to mirror a home nursery, with a crib, small blankets, "lovies," miniature diapers, a diaper-changing table, small bottles, an empty formula container, small bowls and spoons, a doll-sized high chair, small stroller, plenty of clothes hanging in a small wardrobe, table lamps, small toys, board books, and a small rocking chair. This well-developed space, as you can imagine, invites a deep dive into the care of a small human and invites a style of play rich in narrative, joy, social encounter, and life.

Honoring the Role of Aesthetics and Beauty in the Learning Process

What do we mean by aesthetics? While *aesthetics* is often used to describe something that is pretty, our definition includes this idea but goes well beyond that. We believe that the role of aesthetics and beauty in the classroom environment is not a superficial concern but an essential aspect of the learning. It serves as a catalyst in shaping the learning experience. When we pay attention to its power, aesthetics help us create invitations that catch a child's eye and intrigue. If we ignore the aesthetics in an environment wrought with complexity, children walk into a room that is jumbled, messy, and "unreadable." This, of course, works against our goals. However, if a child walks into an environment where there is curation, organization, and beauty in the design, then the space itself is inviting them to think beyond the ordinary and ask questions that spark creativity and imagination. Aesthetics can be multisensorial and help us keep in mind the roles light, smell, color, shape, spacing, and texture can play in creating a robust and pleasing environment or microenvironment.

Intention and Responsiveness to the Needs and Interests of Inhabitants

Educators in Reggio Emilia have spoken about every corner of every space having meaning and purpose. We have found that approach to be a cornerstone of our design process. Spaces are included—or not—with great intention, and the materials within them are also carefully chosen. We begin, as always, with our documentation.

- What patterns have we seen in children's interests and behaviors?
- What conversations are they having?

- What big ideas do they seem to revisit again and again?
- What do the children seem particularly drawn to?
- What are the interests of the adults?
- What do we need to accomplish?
- How can we optimize the natural interests of those involved to accomplish our goals?

All these questions serve as a kind of design research that informs our next steps and decision-making processes. Thus, when we design spaces or classrooms, we are armed with an enormous amount of information and can launch from an empathetic place. We have found that this intentional approach to design and curation is instrumental in the success of the space as it is helps us understand the children and adults who use it, and it supports learning and play at a higher level. Including the children in the design of spaces and selection of materials can also be powerful. In this way, they also have ownership for the use, care, and keeping of the space.

Note that spaces morph and shift, with intention, as the children's interests develop. For instance, we design classrooms each year that include dramatic play, construction, art studios, textile studios, tinkering and maker spaces, light and shadow, messaging, and digital landscapes. Based on what we know about the children entering the class, we choose the size of the space and many of the materials within it. However, if the children have a strong interest in one of these areas, we will shift our design and make the space much larger and even more complex to encourage their work and play. Equally, if not more important, we pay careful attention to the spaces and materials that are not being used. Why aren't they inviting children in? Are the space and its organization "readable" to children? What were we trying to accomplish with them? How might we organize the materials differently? Do the children need the support of a planned provocation to lend possibility? Do we need to try new materials to accomplish the same goals? This is not a flippant, erratic, or fast decision-making process. Nor is it scheduled. Instead, it is a part of the ongoing research in the room and looks different based on the teachers, children, and situations in a classroom.

This year, one of the classes showed a strong interest in clay. We redesigned the room to include a well-developed clay studio and placed clay, in different forms, in several relevant areas of the room to spark thinking and experimentation. For instance, clay next to wire invites different possibilities than clay combined with natural materials does. In another classroom, the children had an intense interest in textiles and sewing. We, along with the children, designed a robust textile studio. In this way, no two rooms are exactly the same, but instead reflective of the interests and personalities of those who live in them. Much like a home situation, each classroom reflects the values of the school but leaves space for the individual identities of the class. This means that there is no prescription for the design of environments. Just as the space remains responsive to children, it also remains responsive to those developing it.

Spaces that Inspire Inquiry and Ignite Adventure

In a school that tries to blur the boundaries between life and the classroom, it is important to honor childhood and its inherent whimsy and playfulness. While we remain committed to the highest quality care and learning contexts, we remain equally committed to protecting the joy of a relaxed childhood. We also embrace the intellectual integrity that young children bring with them. So, with all of this in mind, we aim to create spaces that provoke beautiful questions, differing perspectives, offer trickery and amusement, and require thinking, but only of the most fun and adventurous kind.

Adventure awaits around every corner of childhood. When we embrace it as a cornerstone of learning and living, we embrace the fun of living. We all remember things and experiences that make us laugh. Or the expeditions that uncover magic or beauty.

An adventure for infants can be found on a picnic blanket on a sunny day in the midst of a large field of flowers. For toddlers, it can be a trek across a rocky terrain on their way up a large hill. What is important is the unknown or the expectation that anything wonderful could happen at any moment. It becomes the role of the adults, then, to keep this sense of wonder alive. We can do this by keeping our curiosity thriving, taking time to discover and rediscover alongside the children. We also do this through the kinds of questions we entertain from the children. How do the leaves know when and how to change? What kind of fairies live in the woods? What makes a fairy fat? Are there trolls under every bridge on campus or just a few? What kinds of shoes could a peacock wear in the winter? Are the petals of flowers umbrellas for grasshoppers? Is there a city underground built just for bugs? Does it have a hotel for ants? Do grasshoppers speak in rainbows? Can fireflies understand them? Can snails and butterflies be best friends? When we begin with questions like these, immediately the adventure is underfoot and the spaces, materials, and experiences of a child's day are dedicated to building and testing theories, representing the thinking, and enjoying the pleasures of constructing answers together with their friends.

Beckoning Social Encounters in the Construction of Knowledge

Social constructivist learning harnesses the child's natural curiosity and drive to make sense of the world. Believing that knowledge is not a static entity to be transmitted but a dynamic collaborative creation, we design our spaces to invite children to learn by "actively doing" alongside their friends. As we design and create environments, we are careful to embed the many concepts, paradigms, and domains of learning that we need to uncover. This is different than a more traditional approach and involves a mind shift where the emphasis is on learning instead of teaching. This approach implies a kind of scavenger hunt for all the learning potentials hidden around the room. It also implies that the teacher is hyperaware of the possibilities and is ready to encourage and facilitate the encounters that might ensue.

Our environments are designed to be a sort of beautiful laboratory, where small groups congregate, where the hand and mind work in unison, and where the creative and the cognitive grow side by side. This in turn creates spaces where the hum of learning is palpable and visible through the children's conversations, questions, theories, experiments, observations, actions, and iterations. They are learning from and alongside their friends while at the same time serving as catalysts for their friends' learning. Thus, our environments always include space for small groups and take into account the many ways those groups might interact and explore in the area. They also offer a wide selection of choices, so that there is rarely one right answer but an ongoing unfolding and negotiation, wrought with multiple perspectives and demanding articulation.

When thinking about the design of an environment that honors the role of social encounters in learning, it is imperative to include space, materials, and curated experiences that invite encounter and dissonance, where the unknown is possible but even more possible if children and teachers work together.

Creating innovative, dynamic, and engaging learning environments is an imperative element of curated learning occasions. The complexity and the aesthetics of an experience and intelligent materials foster an attitude of experimentation, problem solving, and the social construction of knowledge. Inherent in this way of thinking is an educator who is responsive to the thinking and actions of the children in their class. They enthusiastically observe and document the actions of the children, and in return, offer complex experiences that support the extension of one experience into the next, thus creating a thread of continuity across experiences and interests while remaining open to new curiosities presented by the children.

Chapter 3:

Teacher Researcher: The Cycle of Observation, Documentation, Analysis, and Projection

"Stand aside for a while and leave room for learning, observe carefully what children do, and then, if you have understood well, perhaps teaching will be different from before."

—Loris Malaguzzi (*The Hundred Languages of Children*, 2011)

We must begin with the *why*. Many visitors to our school wonder, rightfully, how we know what to do next and when to do it, or how we draw conclusions regarding children and their learning. Our answer is remarkably complex, but to begin, it lies within the why. To design and curate interesting environments and scenarios within them, we must know what we are trying to accomplish and why we want to accomplish it. We consider our answers to questions such as the following:

- Who are we designing for?
- On what observed actions or reactions are we basing these choices?
- What big ideas or concepts are we hoping the children uncover?
- What domains of learning do we want to embed?
- What cognitive knots do we want children to encounter?
- In how many interesting ways can that happen?
- With how many and what variety of materials can that happen?
- In what social context can it all take place?

Once we understand the why behind the design and thinking, then we can begin to unpack the what and when. Building answers to these questions is not an easy or simple process. Nor should it be. Deep learning is complex and deserves careful attention.

Mindsets and Dispositions

The mindsets and dispositions of both the children and the educators is paramount to the success of schools like Riverfield. First and foremost is the image of the children and educators as highly competent and capable learners and people. Educators must recognize the children's innate curiosity and consistently cultivate their own. This leads to the educators not only challenging the children but also challenging themselves and creating a culture of thinking, action, and learning. Carol Dweck is an American psychologist who studies the reasons for success. In her book *Mindset: The New Psychology of Success*, she defines two types of mindsets: a fixed mindset and a growth mindset. Having a growth mindset can lead to success and is imperative in Reggio-based education. As Dweck states, "The passion for stretching yourself and sticking to it, even (or especially) when it's not going well, is the hallmark of the growth mindset. This is the mindset that allows people to thrive during some of the most challenging times" (Dweck, 2006).

A growth mindset offers learners the opportunity to take risks, and by taking risks they may at some point experience failure. Maintaining a positive disposition and continuing to persevere are necessary aspects of an attitude of ongoing research. When you include children's interests in their learning, you see them developing a growth mindset, pursuing a passion, and exhibiting grit in their project work. We hope that as children develop these mindsets and dispositions at an early age, they become hallmarks of children's attitudes toward learning and living.

In addition to the growth mindset, an innovator's mindset is also at play for both adults and children. This means that they hold a disposition that embraces the unknown, reflects and responds, navigates ambiguity, and looks in new ways at situations that once held certainty. This approach is different than a mindset that seeks one right answer achieved in one way. Instead, it is a disposition that seeks mystery and magic in the world and finds ways to harness the inquiry and make it palpable. In short, an innovator's mindset seeks new ways of seeing, inventing, and keeping learning and living vibrant and dynamic.

Systems

Layering atop the teachers' mindset, we have also designed systems to support them in careful observation and analysis of the children's unfolding work. It is important to note that we embrace the subjectivity of this process. Each teacher brings their experiences, perspectives, understandings, and relationships; objectivity is an illusion. What we are hoping for in observation is a deep understanding of strategies and tools used in children's quest for knowing. This is not a checklist but an ongoing collection and analysis of children's learning processes made evident through gestures, microgestures, facial expressions, choices, emotions, connections, social references, and so on. Documentation can happen through many strategies: photography, video recording, audio recording, notes, and sketches all serve as tools to capture documentation for later analysis. Observation forms that include aspects of many of these tools are a daily practice in every teacher's repertoire.

Carlina Rinaldi, President of The Foundation of Reggio Children Centro Loris Malaguzzi, Reggio Emilia, has described the documentation process as "a strong act of love and caring" (Rinaldi, 2004), and we have experienced this as true. This active form of listening with all of our senses, recording what we observe for later analysis, and articulation of our findings is at the heart of our daily practice and communicates to children that what they do and say is important and worthy of our time and attention. This then reinforces the children's efforts, intrinsic motivation, and persistence in the face of challenges. Because we have chosen an attitude that holds both children and educators as competent and capable, and we believe school is a place of ongoing research for all, we aim to design and document experiences where children can't help but learn.

In the design of an experience, a teacher considers the social nature of learning and sets up invitations that require children to encounter multiple and differing perspectives, opportunities for testing and negotiating hypotheses and theory, and time and space for both individual and group construction of knowledge. By design, the experiences encourage calculated risk-taking, comfort in "not knowing," and making attempts at something new. Knowing that risk is an essential part of learning, mistakes or unanticipated outcomes are embraced as opportunities for deeper understanding instead of failure. In this way, we can encourage children to develop flexible thinking, resilience, and an attitude of experimentation and research. We can then observe and document their individual and group strategies and attempts. During these experiences, the role of the teacher is multifaceted. Active listening demands the use of all the senses. So, teachers spend time observing the children's actions, interactions, and attempts. They take note of and record children's conversations. They watch and document the dynamics of the group and transcribe the ways in which children contribute to or strategize within the group. They make decisions about how to alter the group dynamic, environment, or curation of materials, if needed, for the next encounter.

Observing and documenting an experience requires practice and patience, a commitment to one's own learning, and confidence in one's own competence and capability. That being said, it is not done in complete isolation. The ongoing collaboration of coteachers, children, families, pedagogical leaders, and embedded professional development serve as strong support and encouragement for educators.

It is not enough, however, to simply compile images and notes; the mere collection of artifacts does not constitute research. In embracing school as an ongoing place of research, we also embrace the collective and collaborative analysis of the trails and traces of work and use them to inform our next steps. Thus, learning how to "read" photographs or video and decipher what children might be thinking, strategizing, or communicating; glean important phrases or words from children's conversations; listen for the nuances in tone and tenor in audio recordings; and find patterns or uncover children's maps of thinking are all skills that we continually develop and refine. It takes practice to interpret the "thinking toes" of an infant, the famous pointing finger of a toddler, or the nuanced gazes of children. However, these skills are imperative if teachers are truly walking alongside the children in their quest for understanding and hope to remain engaged in the research process toward building knowledge.

We embed professional development, both formal and informal, in an ongoing fashion. Just as with children, learning through experience is the most effective strategy to develop skills and construct knowledge that can be applied across situations. Each day, teachers reflect on the collections of notes, imagery, sketches, and artifacts with their coteacher to create a daily journal that is shared with children and emailed to families. Teachers analyze and synthesize their understanding of what happened, why it was important, what it means for future encounters. They articulate their interpretations through imagery and narratives. In this way, teachers are analyzing the learning processes, explaining their choices, and honing their skills for drawing conclusions alongside their team teacher and the children and creating a living memory for all.

At the end of a week or two, teachers, alongside pedagogical coaches, reflect on the collection of daily journals to further analyze and synthesize the learning strategies and encounters. We "read" the collection of images together, openly questioning and challenging assumptions as we look again for what happened, why it was important, and what it means for next steps. We then synthesize the compilation of daily journals into mini stories of learning that highlight the threads of continuity, children's reactions and strategies, teacher's actions, curation of the environment and materials, development in the domains of learning, and the joy of the process. We hang these low on the wall as a guided memory of experience for children, teachers, and families. When thinking about how to move forward, each of the aspects are taken into careful consideration. The interpretations of the children, the pedagogical coaches, and team teachers all help design a repertoire of possibilities teachers can pull from as they move forward, based on their daily observations.

And so it continues: an ongoing collection, analysis, and synthesis followed by articulation and supported by daily reflection on the part of teachers and children. All of which helps teachers choose the next steps. It is a complex and dynamic system that keeps us walking closely alongside children and their curiosities while weaving the domains of learning such as literacy, math, science, and social and emotional learning into designed and curated encounters. It is a self-propelling system that is responsive, agile, and rooted in interesting experience and intentional pedagogy. This system requires full engagement, high levels of thinking, and a commitment to informed action that evolves alongside our understanding of children's joyful construction of knowledge.

Respect for Time

The cycle of inquiry—setting up environments; collecting and organizing intelligent materials; curating occasions for learning; and observing, documenting, and analyzing the children's actions and reactions to inform next steps—takes place over several weeks and many encounters. While each encounter morphs into the next, it is important to understand that time is an imperative consideration and that teachers choose carefully how long a certain provocation remains for the children to revisit, when to walk away for a bit, when to relaunch, and when to begin a transition to something new. "Giving time to time" is an important facet of the process, meaning we are not looking for learning that happens in a superficial manner as a "fly by" encounter and moving according to the pace of outside forces. We are not in pursuit of one right answer; instead, we are looking for situations and occasions that afford rich inquiry, multiple and opposing perspectives, challenge, surprise, enticement, and opportunities to grapple with big ideas. Children experiment and test budding theories and build meaning in their world. This requires time and space.

Elements teachers may consider in navigating timing can include the depth of children's interactions, the variety of strategies an invitation provokes, children's joy, how many new questions arise with each experience, the array of problems or cognitive knots the encounter poses, and the kinds of social interactions that actively encourage the work. In this book, we do not claim to offer an answer, only an experience, and we hope that from this offering you find questions and inspirations that propel your thinking and action in ways that are unique and responsive to you, the children you work with, and the context in which you teach and learn.

The inquiry cycle helps teachers understand the what, when, why, and how of their next steps. They must hone observation, documentation, analysis, and projection skills. Supported by dispositions that include a growth and innovator's mindsets, as well as systems for ensuring time, teachers weave space and practice into the daily life of the classroom. They fine-tune their abilities to read nuances in photographs, pick up tones and word choices in audio recordings, and analyze a series of actions in a video to understand and articulate the learning processes of young children more fully. Through an ongoing cycle of analysis, synthesis, and making the daily life of the classroom visible in observation sheets, journals, panels, wall documentation, and presentations, teachers synthesize the collection of interesting experiences. In this way, teachers walk closely alongside children and their interests to remain provocateurs of further discovery and curated occasions.

Section II:

Invitations and Possibilities: A Diary of Rich Experiences for Infants and Toddlers

Chapter 4: The Color Lab

For our environments to remain responsive to children's interests, we continually design and redesign them in intentional and interesting ways. Therefore, when we observed an ongoing fascination with color, the color lab was born in a common area adjacent to the infant and toddler classrooms. This space further encourages the children's and teachers' action research regarding color, light, tangible vs. intangible, transparency, and transformation.

Colorful Peekaboo

Building on previous experiences in the classroom, these teachers utilized the triangle mirror space in the color lab to investigate how the children would react to an invitation filled with light, color, reflection, and movement. Hanging colorful scarves, rope lights, small moveable light spheres, and crystal balls in an array of colors adorn the space, beckoning the children to manipulate, grasp, roll, share, and engage. Two of the older infants are instantly drawn to the hanging scarves and begin a game of peekaboo. One child intentionally sits behind the row of scarves, obscuring his face with the red one and smiling as if inviting his friend to the game. Another child crawls over to take a closer look. Amused by the way his friend appears behind the scarf, the two begin giggling as the second child reaches to pull the scarf from his friend's face. Through this experience, the innate social nature of very young children shines through, serving as a reminder that the intentionality behind the provocations, the quality and quantity of materials offered, the positioning of children to ensure social connections, and the belief that children

learn in a social context make a difference in the quality of the children's encounter. As the game of peekaboo unfolds, the educators wonder how they might offer experiences in other ways that invite the construction of a game. How can they continue to set up experiences that foster social connections between young children?

Big Ideas and Concepts:

- Game
- Reciprocity
- Light and transparency
- Reflection
- Color
- Shift in perspective
- Dimensionality
- Conversation
- Social intelligence
- Spatial awareness
- Object permanence
- Projection
- Shadow
- The joy of being together

Teachers' Thoughts and Wonderings:

- What about this invitation so strongly invited *game*?
- Is the idea of *game* innate?
- How many other ways can we invite the concept of *game*?
- Will children expand the game beyond two players?
- Will others who previously observed join in the fun?
- Is this a game played at home?
- What attracted these two children, and why did it not attract the other three playing nearby?

Possible Next Steps:

- Revisit the scenario and observe whether the same game ensues.
- Curate a variety of objects that roll to invite a different but familiar game that might include more children.

A Palette of Light and Color

Having observed the children engage in peekaboo in a variety of scenarios, the next invitation provided a possible shift. Placing a wide variety of rollable objects among the materials already introduced, the teachers wonder if a new game might ensue. As the children move into the space, they are welcomed by a palette of lights, both white and colored, alongside clear, colored orbs; reflective spheres; and tall, colorful water bottles lying beneath the favored hanging scarves of various hues. Optimizing the full dimensionality between the floor and ceiling, the space hints at the many possibilities for conversations. Teachers quietly anticipate the children's next move in the adjusted space.

The children, seemingly captivated by the welcoming glow, crawl toward the space with enthusiasm. Once in the midst of possibility, they pause, apparently assessing the situation and perhaps orienting to the new encounter. Some children are drawn to the orbs that shift colors as they touch them. Others are enamored with the string of white lights. Still others are fascinated by the billowing scarves that had previously invited games of peekaboo.

The children's curled toes and thinking tongues indicate that the space holds their full attention as they move from one material to the next, layering their understandings and combining materials in interesting ways. Will the reflective spheres change colors in similar ways to the white orbs? Can the children see themselves and their friends in the colored orbs? Why not? Do all the balls fit in the clear tube? Do they always roll out? What do the balls do in the tube between their entrance and exit? What are my friends doing? How did they do that?

Although teachers entered the experience anticipating a game of rolling or passing the many spheres, they are particularly struck by how many perspectives and cognitive knots are uncovered through the "friendship" between light, color, and reflection.

Big Ideas and Concepts:

- Color
- Transformation of color when light and color meet
- Illumination
- Children's ability to manipulate the light
- Comparison
- Shape
- Size
- Motion
- Conversation
- Weight and density
- Testing
- Space
- Reflection in the metal balls
- The way the light orbs capture the illumination around them

Teachers' Thoughts and Wonderings:

- The addition of the colored orbs overshadowed the invitation of the scarves.
- The game was set aside to research the newly added light orbs.
- In contrast to previous occasions in which the scarves were the main focus, most of the children's attention was focused down toward the palette of illuminated spheres.
- The children are mesmerized by color and illumination.

Possible Next Steps:

- Revisit the concept of *game* with different materials that offer similar outcomes.
- Build a permanent color peekaboo installation.
- Collect translucent colored objects, such as acetate, acrylic, plastic containers, water bottles, and melted plastic pieces.
- Collect interesting opaque materials to invite the cognitive knot between the expected translucence and the surprise of opacity.
- Offer ways for children to capture and/or move light and color.
- Offer projected digital landscapes that immerse the children in large-scale color.

Translucency and Opacity: Peekaboo Revisited

Noticing the children's fascination with the spinning color wheel in the color lab and the ways in which they use the colored triangles as hued windows, the educators sought to challenge the children's understanding of color and opacity. Sometimes we want to reinforce the theories and hypotheses the children are forming. At other times, we want to create provocations that intentionally defy and contradict their proposed theories and hypotheses. On this day, the teachers want to draw attention to the difference between the translucent color wheel and the opaque fabrics of the same colors. Would the children recognize the colors? How would they explore color they could no longer see through?

As the children explored the materials, they seemed initially to be struck by the fluidity and movement of the colored fabric. But soon, the addition of flashlights offered another dimension and helped to highlight the quality of opacity. Translucency took on even more meaning when two children found each other through the colored windows. Much like the prior experience with the colored transparent scarves, the children found joy in the game of peekaboo.

Big Ideas and Concepts:

- Translucent vs. opaque
- The way color shifts based on the opacity or translucence of an object
- Flashlights as a source to control light
- Color mixing
- Fluidity of scarves and fabric
- Game
- Flashlights highlight translucence
- Translucent colored objects offer a colored shadow when light shines through them

Teachers' Thoughts and Wonderings:

- The game returned.
- Multiple players participated.
- The variety of materials supported a variety of iterations of the game.
- There is an intense fascination with flashlights as controllable instruments of light.

Possible Next Steps:

- Incorporate colored shadows in future provocations.
- Add more light sources for the children to manipulate.
- Offer immersive projected light that cannot be manipulated.
- Highlight the possibility that mirrored reflection affords.

Monochromatic Shadows

Discovering a shadow can be a profound experience. A shadow can unveil the hidden presence of an object or person and offers a mystery of origin and connection. Where is it coming from? Why does it move? Can I capture it? Once a child discovers its source, the joy is contagious and can be a springboard for continued inquiry.

In this experience, the children are invited to the mirror box and a projection of green spotlights dancing before them. At first, the children are just fascinated by the colored moving shapes. As the light passes over one child, another notices the shadow made by his friend's image but as yet hasn't made the connection. The game continues and the fascination and joy grow.

One child, who had been watching his friends' engagement from afar and gathering information and building a theory, cautiously ventures in front of the light and watches as his own shadow appears. He seems to notice the parallel between his own movement and the simultaneous movement of his shadow. New connections and new theories are taking root.

By taking away the clutter of detail, shadows distill an object to its simplest form. That simplicity offers to the child an opportunity to delve deeper into the complexity of the interplay between illumination and light and darkness, illusion and reality.

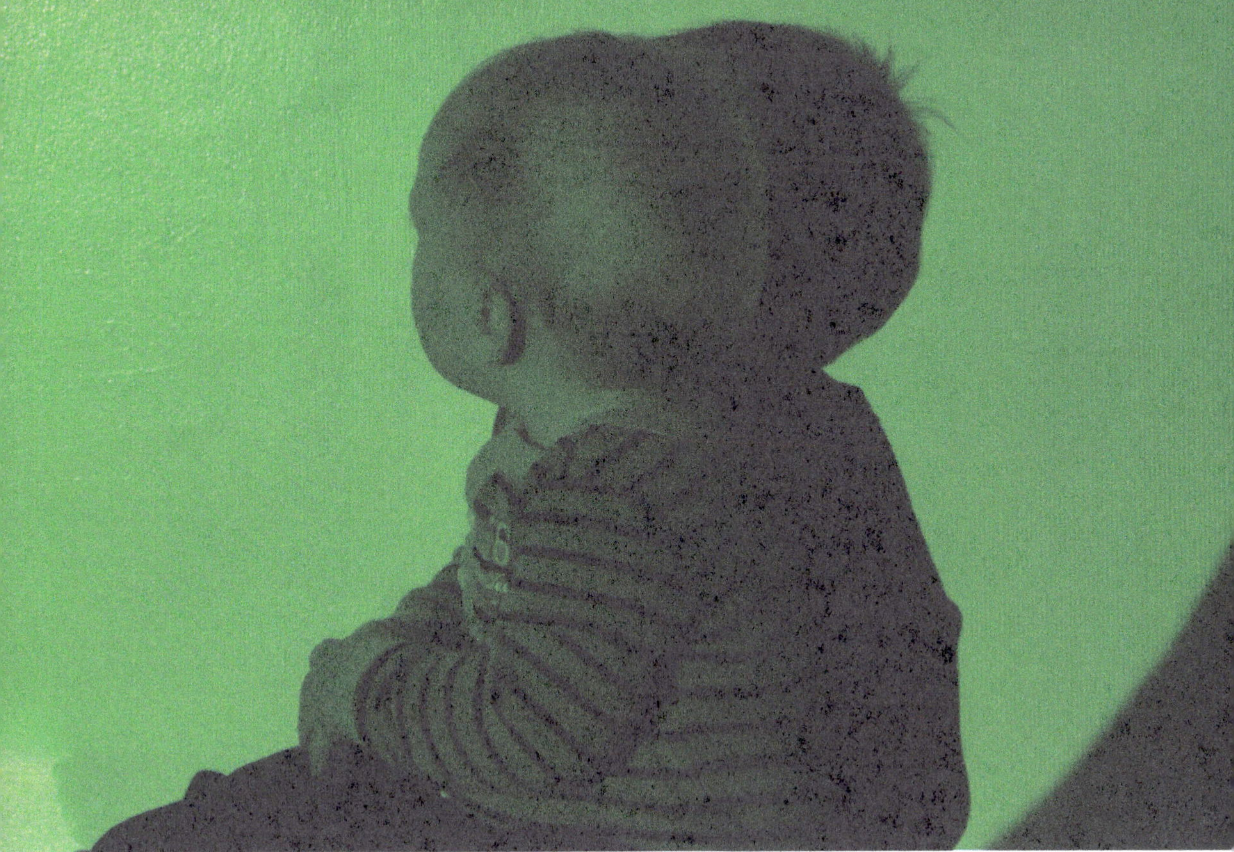

Big Ideas and Concepts:

- Shadow
- Movement of color
- Reflection
- Immersive experience
- Tangible and intangible
- The game of chase
- Scale
- Source of light
- Transformation of perspective when the world is seen through a different hue
- Conversation
- Social exchange

Teachers' Thoughts and Wonderings:

- The game of capturing a shadow and moving color
- The interaction between shadows and moving color
- Children captivated by the immersive nature of projected color
- The novelty of the experience seemed to invite *game*.

Possible Next Steps:

- Add moving color vs. stagnant color projections.
- Add projections of multiple colors mixing.
- Use colored lights to create a game between color and shadow.

Colored Shadow Trickery

Colored shadows are a fascinating optical phenomenon that occur when different colors are cast as shadows, often as a result of multiple light sources or objects with varying hues interacting in complex ways. This phenomenon challenges the intuitive understanding of shadows as being solely black or gray and invites cognitive disequilibrium. After observing the children's happy fascination with the mysteries of shadow, we wondered how we might offer another layer of trickery to their emerging experiments and theories. After researching how we could create this effect, we hung three small, colored spotlights—one red, one blue, and one yellow—to cast layers of colored shadows into the mirrored box.

Upon seeing the invitation for the first time, the children were drawn to the way the colors mixed before them creating shades of pink, purple, green, and teal. When one child felt brave enough to enter the mirrored box, they were delighted to find that their shadows, which they had previously only known as black, were colorful and multidimensional. As they moved about the box, the multiplicity of shadows changed colors as the spotlights mixed in different ways behind them. The educators noticed several children tentatively walking to the far wall of the box and reaching out to touch the shadow before them, as if daring to ask if it was real and tangible. Is this me or not me? Can I control it?

Big Ideas and Concepts:

- Shadow
- Color
- Reflection
- Color mixing
- Shade and hue
- Dimensionality

- Surprise
- Sense of self
- Movement
- Elusive
- Echoes of reality
- Lack of color

Teachers' Thoughts and Wonderings:

- Children seemed to associate their movements with the movements of the shadows.
- The responses to the appearance of multiple shadows
- Light colors mix in interesting and different ways than tangible colors.
- The elusiveness of the shadow captivated children's attention.
- Mystery creates excitement and engagement.
- Large-scale immersive experiences continue to captivate.

Possible Next Steps:

- Create a large-scale immersive occasion that children can manipulate.
- Continue the combinations of tangible and intangible.
- Layer black shadows and colored shadows.
- Consider other ways to create colored shadows.
- Offer large-scale bubbles, color, and immersion.

Symphony of Color, Light, and Scale

An overhead projector is a tool that holds allure for young minds. On this day, adorning the lit glass top with tangible, amorphous plastic pieces painted a large-scale projection of intangible color across the wall. The color composition beckoned a game of trickery and amusement as the children manipulated the objects on the glass and watched as their gestures composed an enchanting invitation of size, depth, distortion, and transformation upon the wall. Taking the pieces off the glass and comparing them to the imagery on the wall, the children made the connection between the tangible and the intangible. But what magic lay inside the projector that allowed the plastic shapes to become so large? Again, technology transforms the ordinary to the extraordinary and invites a layer of complexity that deepens inquiry and exploration. Creating a new disequilibrium with familiar materials and concepts, this experience invited a new perspective, additional queries, and ongoing interest.

Big Ideas and Concepts:

- Color
- Scale
- Hues
- Size
- Manipulation of color
- Color mixing
- Conversation
- Shifts in perspective
- Light projection
- Transformation
- Navigating the unknown
- Problem solving

Teachers' Thoughts and Wonderings:

- Some children were immediately attracted to the overhead projector to manipulate the projections.
- Some children more closely observed the source of the light and manipulated the pieces to move the projected images about the room.
- Some children moved the objects themselves to interact with light and projected large-scale images.
- The children seemed transfixed with the capacity to capture and manipulate the colors of familiar objects transformed and in a larger scale on the wall.
- The ongoing transformation and evolution of their composition brought great joy to the children.

Possible Next Steps:

- Offer occasions that involve movement of color or transformation of what seems certain.
- Add tangible items that can be manipulated against a fixed digital landscape.
- Add ways to capture light and color.
- Create or find rainbows of color.

Colored Digital Landscapes: The Challenge of Tangible and Intangible

The teachers of this toddler class wondered how the children could research the relationships among light, color, and water. What if we placed large vases of water in the mirror box and added a layer of moving, colored projection? How might the children navigate between the tangible and the intangible? What games might the projected imagery provoke? How might the relationships among light, color, movement, reflection, and refraction change in this new environment? What strategies would the children invent to negotiate this new experience?

With the vibrant color dancing on the wall, the children began their research mesmerized by the immersive nature of the colored diffusion and its seemingly endless nature. One child's experiment came in the form of presumably trying to capture the color by dipping his hands in the water as his friend watched. Confused by the absence of color on his friend's hand, the second boy referenced the projected imagery, possibly wondering if the answer to this mystery might be found there. The first child continued dipping his hands in the water, determined to find the color within. After only finding an echo of color in the projected imagery, the second child returned to the vase to continue his research, adopting the hand-dipping strategy of his friend.

Big Ideas and Concepts:

- Fluidity of movement in water
- Dispersion of color
- Speed
- Height and scale
- Altered perspective
- Transformation
- Dimensionality
- Volume
- Refraction
- Reflection
- Game
- Exchange
- Social intelligence
- Problem solving

Teachers' Thoughts and Wonderings:

- Children waited for the passing color, tried to grasp it inside the vases, and kept referring to their hands as if looking for the color that had just been inside the vase.
- Did the children notice the color was not real?
- The addition of water distorted the projection and reflections in unanticipated ways.
- The children reintroduced the game of chase.

Possible Next Steps:

- Offer bubbles as a source for a "capturing" and moving color.
- Create a tangible immersive experience.
- Create a complex curation of projection, tangible, light, color, movement, and shadow.

The Enchantment of Bubbles

Wanting to find a way to capture the joy and fun inherent in play with bubbles, the teachers embarked on a mission to fill the space with light, projection, and bubbles. Using several bubble machines, the room quickly filled with the magical material and the excitement and happiness of the children as they tried to pop, catch, and hold the elusive substance. The children peered intently at the colors dancing and reflecting across the spheres. As the teachers observed, it became evident that the children were familiar with bubbles; however, the immersive nature of the experience sometimes caused the children to pause as if trying to decipher whether the heaps of bubbles in front of them were the same thing as the singular bubbles they could catch on their hands. Also of note was the way the projection of moving bubbles and color altered the children's investigation. Initially drawn to the bubbles themselves, as the layers of projection were added—some moving, some shifting the color of the studio—the children were drawn to the reflections made within the bubbles. They explored the flittering shadows the bubbles created across the studio walls and the ways in which they could alter the piles of bubbles by the sweep of a hand or the kick of a leg.

Big Ideas and Concepts:

- Bubble
- Multiplicity
- Movement
- Game
- Refraction and reflection
- Interaction between bubbles and light
- Tangible immersion
- Transformation of color
- Shadow
- Transformation of light depending on the surface it hits
- Delicate
- Tangible yet fleeting
- Capture
- Weight
- Pop
- Size
- Speed
- Mystery
- Conversations
- Cognitive knots
- Joy of being together
- Object permanence

Teachers' Thoughts and Wonderings:

- The creation of a tangible immersive experience afforded close observation of the light created in the bubbles.
- The collection of colors on the surfaces of bubbles dances in the presence of light.
- Children notice the colors.
- Children are surprised by the fleeting nature of a bubble.
- The power to pop was welcomed.
- The combination of tangible and digital immersion mesmerizes children.
- The ability to move the bubbles was a fascination.
- The attention of the children, while mainly focused on bubbles, was also pointed at the large-scale reflections.
- The children seemed surprised by the lack of weight in a bubble. Perhaps they perceived it first as a small ball?

Possible Next Steps:

- Add a bubble blower.
- Offer bubbles in combination with more permanent spheres.
- Add color to the bubble solution.
- Add an overhead projector so that the bubbles that land on the surface are projected large on the wall or ceiling.
- Offer the addition of wind alongside bubbles and spheres.
- Add a musical score that might mirror the tempo and attitude of bubbles.

Continued Inquiries

How does an experience in an immersive environment enhance the properties and characteristics of the material being explored? What roles do reflection and refraction play in this experience?

How does the combination of bubble and shadow create an altered experience? The color lab and the varied experiences within it invite Riverfield's infants and toddlers to construct working definitions of color in far more complex ways than a box of crayons can. The space affords opportunities for color to be fluidly integrated as the children are invited to experiment with big ideas and concepts. Educators continuously invite learning through the organization and presentation of intelligent materials.

Ever responsive, this space will continue to evolve as our understanding and work unfolds. It has become another space in our environment that reminds us of Loris Malaguzzi's words, "The wider the range of possibilities we offer children, the more intense will be their motivations and the richer their experiences" (Edwards, Gandini, and Forman, 2011). We believe the message of this quote is imperative in cultivating a rich and dynamic culture of thinking.

To remain responsive to children's interests, we continually design and redesign environments in intentional and interesting ways. This chapter unpacks the strategies and approaches teachers use to curate complex invitations for children in an infant and toddler color lab. Paying attention to the space from the ceiling to the floor, as well as the floor up, teachers introduce a variety of materials and lightscapes that afford opportunity to experiment with varying textures and sizes of materials, mirrors and their optical illusions, color, light, digital landscapes, tangible vs. intangible, transparency, and transformation. The dance between light and color fascinates the children, altering their perspectives and creating games with transparency and illusion, hide-and-seek, illumination and peekaboo. In addition to the textured color palettes bathed in various light symphonies, digital landscapes beckoned children to play. Unpacking green through an LCD-projected image, moving in rhythm with quiet paint explosions, or walking bear style alongside their color-bathed silhouettes, children played tag with a bubble of light or charades with their shadow. Teachers observed math concepts such as size, scale, color, and pattern, as well as *game*, turn taking, reciprocity, language, large-motor movement, and problem solving, But most importantly, the complexity and aesthetic of the well-curated moments beckoned children's curiosity, engagement, and joy.

mommy
loves me

Chapter 5:

Color Lab Extensions: Reciprocity of Experiences

"When experiences are layered and evolve over time, children are able to build on knowledge, on past experiences, and on emerging understandings. This, in turn, invites them to participate more fully and is one of many ways we can encourage the competent child."

—Alison Maher,
Visionary Director, Boulder Journey School

Echoes of Color: Color Shadows and Hide-and-Seek

Wondering how natural light could affect the dance of color and light, we moved water bottles, each tinted with food coloring, from the color lab to the infant-toddler playground as an open invitation. Beneath the bright sun, the series of rainbow-colored bottles cast their vibrant refractions on the patio. The combination of the tangible water bottles and their intangible refractions produced curiosity and invited further research for the children. Fascinated, a particular child used the ever-important pointing finger to scrape the ground, seemingly in an attempt to capture the color. When the hues fell upon her finger and hand, she lifted her finger in search of the traces of color that had been present moments before. As the color eluded her, she grasped the bottle as if trying to locate the color that had escaped her in a game of hide-and-seek.

We wondered how else we might play the game of capturing elusive color. How could we invite movement of color to play? What other materials could we find to encourage children's research? How many other ways could we interact with the interplay between light and color?

Big Ideas and Concepts:

- Color
- Reflection
- Refraction
- Game: hide-and-seek
- Light: artificial vs. natural
- Intangible
- Distortion
- Perspective
- Shadow
- Color spectrum
- Variation
- Hues
- Series
- Classification
- Mystery
- Elusiveness
- Effects of natural light on color
- Capture
- Dimension
- Gradation
- Nuance

Teachers' Thoughts and Wonderings:

- The ways natural light makes the colors dance on the patio
- Varying strategies for responding to the mystery of the color
- Apparent preference for blue and green over other colors
- The game of hide-and-seek emerges.
- With the water bottles, the children understood the source of the color in front of them, but they did not have the same response to the hued panel.
- Interest in manipulating the bottles to move and attempt to capture the light

Possible Next Steps:

- Create small panels of shades of color that children can hold and manipulate.
- Offer individual color panels to see if the children layer colors to create new colors.
- Move the water bottles inside to see how artificial light shifts the color.
- Because the children are drawn to the blues and greens, consider using a peacock as inspiration for our next steps.

Encounters with the Peacocks

As the unofficial mascots of Riverfield, the freely wandering peacocks provide endless inspiration for the children and the educators alike. Drawing on the natural beauty of the peacocks' feathers, the educators set out to create a series of invitations that incorporated the essence of the peacock with a variety of atelier materials. Over several weeks, the youngest students at Riverfield explored light and color using colored water bottles in a light box. Surrounded by images of their feathered friends and their plumes, and grouped in front of a light box filled with the colors of the peacock, the children manipulated the bottles. As the children pulled the bottles from the holes, the color morphed into something different than it had just been. Through their intent gazes, small moments between friends, and microgestures, it was clear the children were mesmerized by both the glowing color and its transformation as it darkened before their eyes.

Building on the experience in the light box, the educators wondered how a digital peacock, projected atop a white pallet and layered with various fabrics, papers, and ribbons representing the colors of the peacock—as well as actual feathers from the school's peacocks—could further deepen the children's understanding of peacock-ness. Initially drawn to the heaps of fabrics, the children manipulated the materials by pulling, stretching, mounding, and crumpling. As they peeled back the layers of materials, the children were surprised to uncover the moving projection of the peacock. Shifting their curiosity from the tangible materials to the intangible projection, the children reached, pinched, and patted the image of the familiar bird. The children's squeals and shrieks made it evident that the children recognized their beloved peacock. In this experience, the children made clear to the educators that their interest was tied more directly to the peacock himself than to just the colors of the peacock. Accepting this challenge, the educators wondered how they could optimize this fascination and shifted their attention to an outdoor experience in hopes of inviting a chance encounter between the peacock and the children.

Knowing that learning is deepened each time an experience is translated, and fully embracing the children's interest, we decided to explore how an outdoor painting experience would enhance and alter the colors of the peacock. As if waiting for his cue to enter the invitation, the peacock strutted onto the scene and proudly displayed his quills. Using the peacock as a reference point, the children gently dipped their fingers in the paint and traced them across the paper. Noticing the marks their fingers made, the children were amused by their ability to transform the canvas and continued to add to their creation. Throughout these experiences, the teachers wondered how the peacock might provide further inspiration for future invitations. How can we continue to incorporate the tangible materials of the atelier with the intangible digital experiences? How does the use of a familiar image enrich the exploration of unfamiliar materials?

Big Ideas and Concepts:

- Reciprocity between indoors and out
- Digital landscapes
- Texture
- Color
- Sound
- Transparency
- Opacity
- Size
- Comparison
- Tangible
- Intangible
- Echoes of reality
- Paint and paintbrushes
- Natural world
- Friendship
- Connection
- Relationship
- Light
- Shades and hues of blue, green, and purple

Teachers' Thoughts and Wonderings:

- The peacock is a viable explanation as to why the children are drawn to blue and green.
- The children appear to recognize the digital image of the peacock as the same peacock from the day before.
- The children reference each other when unsure, highlighting the social construction of knowledge.

- The blue and green bottles continue to be their preferred choices.
- The children are intrigued by the feather.
- There is still fascination with the light shining through the clear, colored plastics and the shadows they create.
- The children searched for the source of light.

Possible Next Steps:

- Offer flashlights with blue and green cellophane over the lights so the children can manipulate the color.
- Use large mirrors to capture, move, and reflect light, creating additional mystery.
- Use small, handheld, unbreakable mirrors so children can capture, move, and reflect light.
- Offer other materials from the atelier.
- Create other ways for the children and the peacock to have encounters.
- Create an immersive experience with the peacock.
- Find other sources of their favorite shades and hues in nature.

Optical Wonders: Uncovering Reflection, Refraction, and Diffraction

Stepping onto a bridge layered with CDs hanging across the handrails and mirrors covering the planks beneath them, the children entered a world of optical wonders. As the reflections danced across the bridge, the children were captured by both the bouncing reflections and refractions of light and color created by the spinning discs. The radiant and ever-changing hues caused the children to pause. They took time to ponder, seeming to wonder how the colors got there and whether they could make more. The children scratched and tapped the colors as if trying to decipher where they came from and how they could clinch them. With each jump of the colored refraction or reflection, the children followed, resulting in an enthusiastic and elusive hunt.

Moving into the indoor studio with the same invitation, the educators wondered how artificial light would change the way the CDs and mirrors refracted and reflected the light. Would the colors join in the play or remain hidden? Would the same hunt for the elusive rainbows begin? Would the mirrors multiply the colors infinitely?

Inside the studio space, the children repeated their behaviors on the bridge. This time, however, the children were drawn to the origins of the dazzling colors rather than the reflections and refractions produced. Did the CDs hold the key to unlocking this mystery? By moving the CDs, turning them over, and spinning them on their sides, the children tested their hypotheses and emerging theories. Through this manipulation, the children seemed to make clear to the educators that their interest in the concepts of reflection and refraction was far from over. Capitalizing on this interest, the educators wondered how the children could represent their discoveries through the materials of the atelier. Offering a projection of the rainbow of color atop a CD-shaped canvas and a wide spectrum of colorful paints, the educators stepped back to observe as the children experimented with the new medium. Carefully dipping their fingers and paintbrushes in the paint and then grazing them across the canvas, the children watched in amazement as their traces left marks. The children seemed to check between the projection in front of them and the physical CDs surrounding them as if to see if the marks they were making depicted the refraction of the light. Moving forward, the educators wondered what other materials could support the children in uncovering the properties of reflection and refraction, and whether exploration with prisms might offer a similar experience.

Big Ideas and Concepts:

- Diffraction
- Reflection
- Refraction
- Light
- Spectrum
- Movement
- Capture and movement of light
- Manipulation
- Effects of wind
- Multiplicity
- Artificial vs. natural light
- Shadow
- Transformation
- Mark making
- Hues
- Projection
- Elusive
- Rainbow

Teachers' Thoughts and Wonderings:

- The children brought the knowledge from their previous experiences and applied it in this novel situation.
- They easily transitioned between the invitation outside and the invitation inside, and appeared to see the connection by building on the actions they had used before.
- The children were very curious about the rainbow spectrum.
- The reflections of the CDs also interested them.
- The movement of the colors created by the CDs was of particular interest.
- The children connected the image of a rainbow on the CD with the paint colors that surrounded them.

Possible Next Steps:

- Create an immersive experience with bubbles, in which the rainbow is captured and moves.
- Combine CDs with silver mylar balloons and fans to capture and move light and color.
- Combine CDs with reflective spheres to capture and move light and color.

Colors Magnified

As this group of children walked our campus, the teachers noticed the children's fascination with flowers and wondered how this fascination might be harnessed to explore different viewpoints. A thread began weaving its way throughout this particular class: micro- and macroperspectives. To gain a better understanding of the concepts of magnification, the teachers invited a group of children into a garden where magnifying glasses and digital microscopes beckoned. Approaching the invitation with glee and deep respect, the children carefully placed flowers under the digital microscope and magnifying glasses to gain different viewpoints of the minute details of each petal and leaf. How does the perspective of the flower change when viewed through a digital microscope? What about a magnifying glass? Eager to share their discoveries with each other, the children moved seamlessly between the garden full of real flowers and the magnified versions, taking note of the intricacies that each petal presented. As the children continued their research, the educators wondered how the micro- or macroperspective might shift the children's observations of the flowers. Would the shift in perspective affect the attention to detail in the children's representational drawing? What other games might the children create in a digital landscape? How are they similar to or different from the games they create in the tangible world?

What connections are the children making between the tangible and the intangible? How do digital experiences contribute to the child's disposition as a digital citizen?

Big Ideas and Concepts:

- Perspective
- Nature
- Color
- Magnification
- Detail
- Slowing down
- Micro vs. macro
- Nuance
- Texture
- Growth
- Decomposition
- Flower garden
- Digital photography
- New kind of projection
- Mysteries of technology
- Conversation
- Complexity of nature

Teachers' Thoughts and Wonderings:

- The children noticed the intricacies and nuances of each flower.
- They are adept at working the digital microscope.
- They understand the shift in perspective from what they place under the microscopic lens and what is projected on the computer screen.
- They created compositions on the digital microscope pallet.
- They clearly drew a connection between the magnification of a digital microscope and a magnifying glass, which is a more familiar tool.

Possible Next Steps:

- Use the photography the children captured from this experience in combination with materials from the atelier, such as wire, paint, clay, collage, or sketching.
- Use images they collected as digital backdrops in construction or in the studio.
- Introduce new tools to play with the macro- and microperspectives, such as webcams or the zoom feature on digital cameras.
- Create small worlds.
- Create a large-scale painted canvas that represents the essence of the photographs they took.

The Riddle of Shapes without Color

After observing the children's many interactions with color, we wondered how we could create a landscape devoid of color. What if we shifted the color lab into a black box? Then, how might we play with black, white, light, and movement? How would reflection morph within this environment? How would the digital layer add complexity and change perspective? How would the absence of color highlight contrast, reflection, and projection in new ways? We began with a moving digital layer of black and white funhouse shapes in a space

made of black curtains. The children were enraptured by the contrast and the motion of the inverted shadows, at first sitting motionless as they processed what happened before them and then seemingly trying to capture the swirling shapes. The stark antithesis of color inspired a game of chase and tag among friends and the shifting intangible shapes. We wondered what materials we could add that would inspire the children to use tangible shapes in the game.

Big Ideas and Concepts:

- Contrast
- Pattern
- Movement
- Projection
- Shifting reality
- Immersive
- Geometry
- Perspective
- Shifting pattern
- Absence of color
- Light and lack of light
- Capture
- Inverted shadows
- Puzzle
- Riddle
- Cognitive dissonance

Teachers' Thoughts and Wonderings:

- At the beginning, the children were remarkably still, mesmerized by the shifting shapes and trying to orient themselves.
- A common strategy was to try and pick up the shapes or interrupt the motion.

- The children referenced each other for answers to the riddle before them.
- Could the lack of color be mildly disorienting?
- Did the immersion in black help orient or disorient the children?

Possible Next Steps:

- Add tangible geometry and shapes.
- Add a mirror so the projection is above and below the children.
- Integrate shadow.
- Invite the children to build up using construction materials.

The Conundrum Continues

Adding a mirror pallet and curating white and black construction materials atop it, we wondered if the game of "building up" could afford encounters with merging the digital layer and the tangible layers of shape. We were also intrigued by the confusion and amusement that the reflected projection image proposed by dancing across the ceiling. The children, first mesmerized by the infinite nature of the projection in the mirror below them, soon discovered it also floated above. They were immediately captured by this mystery and sat nearly motionless for long periods of time as they watched a familiar series of images from a new perspective. The materials, carefully selected and displayed, were left mostly untouched minus a possible attempt to connect the material to the projection through an outstretched arm. We were struck by how disorienting and fascinating a projection became by simply flipping its location and orientation, and we wondered in what other ways we could play with height, movement, and immersive experiences.

Big Ideas and Concepts:

- Depth
- Height
- Reflection
- Flipped orientation
- Construction
- Dimension
- Scale
- Interaction
- Connection
- Vastness
- Conundrum

Teachers' Thoughts and Wonderings:

- The children again sat almost motionless, seemingly orienting themselves to the situation.
- Their interest was not on the materials in front of them as we expected. Instead, they focused on the projection above. One child tried to connect one of the materials with the projection above, combining the white material with the projection.

- The children noticed the shadows dancing across the white construction materials.
- The darkness seemed to highlight the vastness between the floor and the ceiling.

Possible Next Steps:

- Offer ways to connect the floor and the ceiling.
- Add black, white, and reflective materials that might capture the projection midway between ceiling and floor.
- Add a wind tunnel for different kinds of motion and the ability to reach high.
- Would floating mylar balloons capture and move the image in new and interesting ways?

Connecting Experiences: Intentional Threads of Continuity

As we analyzed and interpreted the children's curiosity about height, we wondered if the wind tunnel, a clear, pivoting tube attached to a small fan that can launch materials at various angles into the air, could empower children to send materials up. First, offering black, white, and reflective materials so that the focus remained on elevation, we watched as the children experimented with the power of wind, weight, and trajectory. The addition of the wind tunnel appeared to balance the children's attention between the intangible projection and the tangible materials. First experimenting with the textiles and then with the materials' capacity for flight, the children were awestruck by the discovery of launch, loft, and altitude. What determines the flight path of a piece of material? What determines the "float" path to the ground? How many materials can take flight at once? All of these inquiries seemed to come to the forefront as the children tucked fabrics into the tunnel and propelled them into the air. As we watched the children play and research the power of wind, we began to wonder how we might be able to further support the construction of answers to their inquiries. Could colored scarves highlight flight and fall in new ways? Would the vibrant contrast leave trails and traces less evident than those of the floating white and black fabrics?

Big Ideas and Concepts:

- Height
- Elevation
- Wind
- Weight
- Trajectory
- Textiles
- Capacity for flight
- Launch
- Loft
- Altitude
- Flight path
- Float
- Propulsion
- Excited inquiry
- Kinesthetic learning
- Whole-body movement

Teachers' Thoughts and Wonderings:

- The children were eager to bridge the floor and the ceiling.
- The unexpected propulsion brought great joy.
- They were equally intrigued by shooting things into the air and watching them float down.
- This was a full-body experience for the children.
- The darkness didn't feel so still with the addition of textiles and wind.
- Would the addition of color in this black space shift the game?
- How might we add color without taking away the power of contrast?

Possible Next Steps:

- Add colored textiles.
- Create shifts in projection.
- Add colored lights.
- Add flashlights.

Reinventing Color to Play

The children met the vivid, sheer scarves beneath the wind tunnel and atop the mirror pallet with excitement. Researching both their translucency and capacity for flight, the children peered through the sheaves of fabric before launching them through the wind-filled chute. With the effect of a rainbow blur, fabric shot out of the tube and wafted to the ground, landing in a crumpled heap. The flight path of color, juxtaposed with the black backdrop, offered brilliant traces of trajectory and descent. As always, the social nature of learning was alive as the children laughed and played with concepts. The shape-shifting forms of fabric in flight magically disrupted the defined edges of the projected geometric shape and the interplay of light, projection, pattern, movement, and color. Translucency created a dissonance that compelled the children's inherent drive to further question, discover, and make meaning of the world around them.

It is not often that teachers of very young children embrace concepts of flight, trajectory, laws of motion, opacity, and translucency, nor do they always move beyond naming color to dive deeply into the plethora of ways color brings meaning and vibrancy to life. This series of experiences, spanning several weeks and supported by a robust environment, intelligent materials, and curious teachers offered a deep dive into the impact of both color and an environment devoid of it. It also afforded opportunities to introduce new materials, concepts, and paradigms as we carefully observed and interpreted the children's actions. The children, fully engrossed in their research, were blissfully unaware of the learning being constructed or of the big concepts, but we were acutely aware of all of this and fully embraced the possibilities and opportunities these concepts provided for thinking, curiosity, discovery, and joy.

Big Ideas and Concepts:

- Vivid
- Sheer
- Contrast between color and black
- Translucency
- Fluid movement
- Descent
- Trajectory
- Tangible shape shifting
- Disruption
- Laws of motion

Teachers' Thoughts and Wonderings:

- The vibrant contrast was as appealing but less disorienting than the previous black and white contrast. Could this be because their world has been so vibrant with color?
- Wind, trajectory, descent, and joy seem to walk hand in hand.
- The children's verbal and physical reactions were louder once color was included.

Possible Next Steps:

- Find other ways to play with the contrast of a black room filled with vibrant color.
- Consider adding a digital landscape of a coral reef.
- Consider adding images of tropical birds or tree frogs.
- Provide images of the works of famous artists and their use of contrast.
- Offer experiences with vibrant materials from the studio, such as collage, paint, wire, glaze, or tape.

In our experience, we find that layering experiences, each time with an added twist, enhances and deepens the learning encounters of the children. When choosing to research the tangible and the elusive, the reciprocity of the indoors and out, and the absence of color vs. color—among other topics—the educator makes informed decisions about what to document, why that specific element is important to highlight, and in what ways they can alter the experience the next time. In curating these rich experiences, children and educators together engage in action research and high-level thinking, creating pathways and strategies for a lifetime of learning.

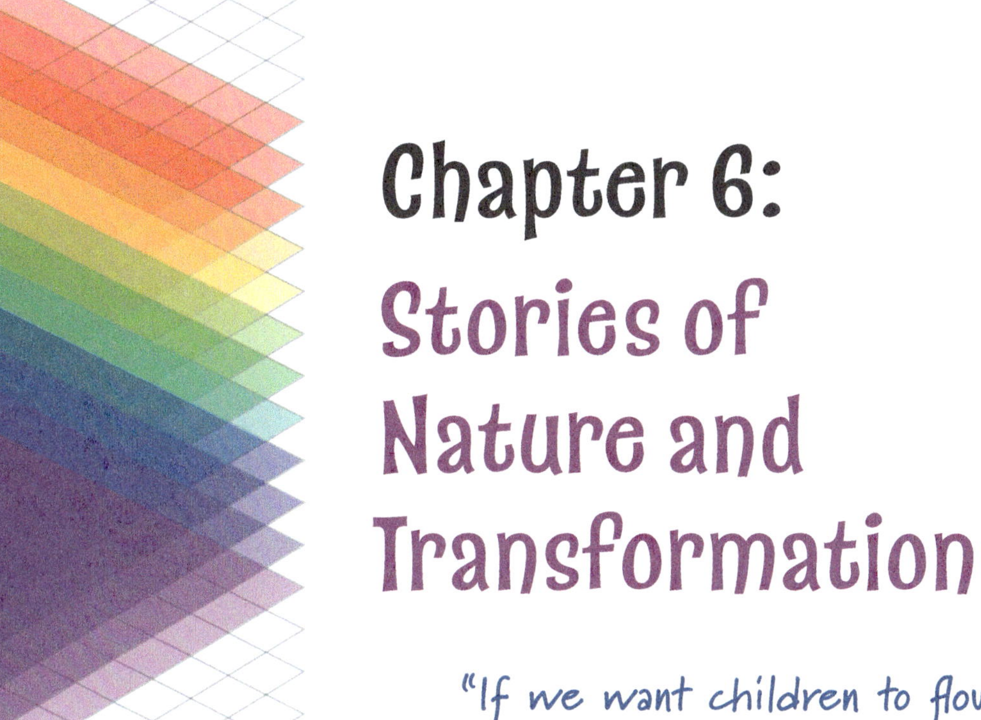

Chapter 6: Stories of Nature and Transformation

"If we want children to flourish, to become truly empowered, let us allow them to love the earth before we ask them to save it."

—David Sobel (2024)

Situated on a 120-acre campus surrounded by wooded trails, a pond, a creek, a barnyard, and freely wandering peacocks, Riverfield embodies adventure in the natural world. Children find joy in the rustling leaves, listen for stories from the bubbling brook, and share secrets with the fluttering butterflies. For them, every tree is a ladder to the sky, and every flower holds the key to magic. Nature offers treasures to be discovered, metaphors to uncover, and adventures on which to embark. From climbing swinging vines to hiking the creek bed or summiting the "Big Hill," we optimize the learning potential and enjoyment that can be found on our vast acreage. The following stories highlight the ways in which nature serves as a joyful and dynamic working laboratory for children and their unfolding research.

Picnic Blanket Laboratory

Knowing that color does not exist in a vacuum, and respecting the children's right to connect their learning to real-life experiences, we regularly optimize the unique and vibrant affordances of color in nature. In one particular year, our campus offered us an intriguing context to further our color research: a field enveloped with yellow flowers. Alongside many explorations in the classroom and color lab, the teachers of the infant class planned several expeditions to the blooming field. Immersed in the vast field, and situated on a blanket with their friends, children began exploring the textures, hues, and details of both individual blooms and clumps of flowers. With careful attention, they delicately manipulated the petals, stems, and leaves, perhaps taking inventory of the nuances in texture, size, color, shape, and smell. The collective inquiry seemed contagious and the picnic blanket laboratory compelling as the children moved with calculated and delicate movements to research the mysteries that surrounded them. As we watched them, we wondered:

- Where could joy, fascination, and surprise be found in this unexpected experience?
- How could we study color through both the grandeur of the field and the tiny details of a single flower?
- In what ways does the immersion in nature, full of sensory experiences, enhance the experience with color and texture?
- How does natural light affect the children's working definition of color?
- What elements were the children drawn to?
- How did they rely on each other to support their experiences in the field?
- What strategies would the children invent for their study?
- What other experiences could we create to extend the children's encounter with shades and hues of yellow and green and the effects light and wind might have?

Careful observation, attention to detail, and shared discovery among friends supported the life and energy of the "wow" in this surprising invitation and reminded us of artist Édouard Manet's words: "There are no lines in nature, only areas of colour, one against another" (Manet, n.d.).

Big Ideas and Concepts:

- Texture
- Size
- Color
- Shape
- Smell
- Breeze
- Sway
- Shared experience
- Collective inquiry
- Delicate
- Sunlight
- Strategy
- Navigating the unexpected

Teachers' Thoughts and Wonderings:

- The children were comfortable as they sat amongst flowers almost as tall as they are.
- Their curiosity was visible through facial expressions, vocal sounds, outstretched hands, and bouncing feet.
- The children referenced their friends for cues on how to proceed.
- A sense of calm existed throughout the experience.
- The children appeared to notice the colors as they reached for the blooms and rolled the petals in their fingertips.

Possible Next Steps:

- Add more ways to manipulate and play with yellow and green.
- Explore a wide range of hues in yellow and green.
- Add artificial light.
- Invite the children to discover yellow and green outside of nature.
- Provide ways to further explore the dance between light and color.

Infant Game of Light, Color, and Transparency

Always looking for ways to highlight the reciprocity between the indoors and out, we wondered how we could combine the colors of the field of flowers with the materials in the indoor color lab. We attempted to recreate the hues of the field within the large color-bottle filled light box that sits on the floor of the color lab. Having transitioned the colors of the water bottles to colors that resembled the hues of the blooming fields, we invited the children to explore alongside their friends. Drawn to the illuminated bottles of colored water, the children accepted the invitation. Seemingly enamored by the soft glow of green, yellow, and orange hues and the ways in which the shades shifted as the children moved the position of their heads, the infants began exploring the colored water bottles. Their preference for yellow was obvious in their reaches and gazes. Could they perhaps be drawing on their previous ventures to the fields of yellow flowers?

Once satisfied with their observation of yellow, the children began manipulating the bottles of green and orange color. One child created a game of shifting shades by first rotating and then pulling the bottle in and out of the light box. This game served as an invitation for a nearby friend to explore in a similar way, creating a beautiful moment of shared discovery. We wondered whether a box full of colored water bottles would offer a new avenue for exploring color. How many combinations of these colors could we make? How could light and color play together to extend the children's experience? How many variations of light, color, and transparency could we create?

Big Ideas and Concepts:

- Illumination
- Light and color
- Translucence
- Shifting shades and hues
- Yellow
- Shared discovery
- Combination
- Pervasive nature of color

Teachers' Thoughts and Wonderings:

- Children's gazes and outstretched arms reached for yellow first.
- Children quickly discovered they could remove and replace the water bottles.
- Children discovered the small bottle's capacity to roll.
- This was a very social encounter.
- There were lots of vocalizations.
- There was serenity in the moment.

Possible Next Steps:

- Add large vases of colored water with light shining through.
- Create a maze of color with towering vases, providing interesting pathways for children to move through.
- Creating a foam core "white box" and capture the "colored shadows" on white foam core while moving the light sources to different distances away or different angles.

A Study in Yellow Flowers with Two-Year-Olds

For several days, the children ventured to the field of yellow flowers with curiosity and excitement. As they trekked across campus to find the phenomenon of an expansive blanket of delicate blooms, we observed children's actions and reactions: "Sun do it," and "So many," accompanied by shrugged shoulders, raised eyebrows, and pointing fingers. We interpreted their reactions as inquiries such as, "How did the flowers get there?" "Did the sun or the wind create them?" "Why are there so many?"

Capitalizing on the curiosities of the children and interested in combining rich experiences in nature with robust materials, we wondered if a table full of flowers gathered by the children from previous outings, watercolors mirroring the colors of the field, and varying sizes of brushes and paper would provoke the children to engage with the field in new ways. Taking time to pause before the encounter, the teacher conversed with the children, encouraging their whimsical wonderings and thoughtful hypotheses before introducing the surprise they would find in the field that day. The children were enamored with what they found and eagerly began work. As they gently swept their brushes across the paper, they could be heard wondering if the fairies of the forest might have left such a magical invitation, or perhaps the peacocks? They could also be heard narrating their observations—comparing

and contrasting the colors or textures on their canvases to the colors and textures of the blooming field. But most importantly, the children and their teachers enjoyed a beautiful and relaxed occasion together as they laughed, talked, painted, and played in a world bursting with color and surprise. Once again, the lines between school and life, thinking and beauty, joy and learning blurred.

Big Ideas and Concepts:

- An occasion for gathering
- Shared experience
- Blooming
- Wildflower fields
- Hues of yellow and green
- Height
- Abundance
- Vast space
- Varying texture
- Watercolor
- Paintbrush
- Mark making
- Pause
- Observation
- Growth of a flower
- Sounds of nature
- Friendship

Teachers' Thoughts and Wonderings:

- The children paused when they sat at the table, seemingly taking in the nuances and complexities that surrounded them.
- We perceived magic in the moment.
- The children gave the peacock and fairies credit for creating the field of flowers.
- The children drew connections between the field they were in and the watercolors and verbalized these connections with words or simple sentences.
- The children worked with intention and had varying strategies for applying paint to the brush and the paper.

Possible Next Steps:

- Provide materials for large-scale painting.
- Invite encounters with other materials from the atelier, such as chalk pastels, oil pastels, wire, clay, or collaged composition.
- Invite games through the use of mirrors laid in the field for altered perspectives.
- Offer encounters with a variety of yellow flowers, such as sunflowers, carnations, and gerbera daisies.

Large-Scale Interpretations with Two-Year-Olds

Returning again to the field of yellow flowers, the two-year-old children were eager to see what surprises awaited them. They found large easels and paint carts with shades and hues of yellow and green curated days before in the classroom. Intrigued by the large-scale easels, the children began creating interpretations on the paper with big gestures. As they began painting, it was interesting to watch as they employed various strategies. One child was drawn to a shade of paint that matched his shirt. He carried it to the easel and held on to it tightly as he made his marks. A few children moved between the paint cart and the easel, experimenting with different colors and sizes of paintbrushes. Others experimented with the vastness of the canvas and the variety of large movements it invited. As they moved about, the children shared the space, paints, and paintbrushes with ease. Some children chose to work independently, while others gathered around one easel in a collaborative effort. Using the field around them as inspiration, the children examined the flowers closely to ensure they captured the details of the flowers, sharing their findings with each other along the way. Throughout this encounter, the educator stepped back to document through photography, and listened intently to the conversations between the children to determine what invitations she could offer to the children that would continue to capture their interest and build on the excitement the children had while working in the field of yellow flowers.

Big Ideas and Concepts:

- Large scale
- Inspiration
- Interpretation
- Abstract
- Metaphor
- Representation
- Intentionality
- Height
- Space
- Dimension
- Easel painting
- Strategy
- Permanence
- Interconnectedness
- Life
- Sky
- Sun
- Wind
- Easel
- Paint
- Paintbrush
- Line
- Shades and hues
- Joy of being together
- Shared experience
- Beauty and serenity of being outdoors

Teachers' Thoughts and Wonderings:

- Children chose hues and shades of colors with intention.
- Some chose to work independently at an easel; others chose to cluster and share an easel and its canvas.
- The children responded to the large space with big gestures.
- Children chose the size of the paintbrush intentionally. They altered which paintbrush they used based on what they were representing.
- The joy of being together was pervasive.
- The shared experience offered courage to those that were hesitant.
- Many of the children paused several times to look around them before continuing with the next color or paintbrush.
- Some children chose paint colors based on their shirt or sock colors.
- The children settled into the experience easily and stayed working for an extended period of time (more than thirty minutes).

Possible Next Steps:

- Provide one large (6–8 feet long) easel and four or five paint carts filled with paint colors.
- Revisit the paintings again many times to add more color, various kinds and widths of lines, and so on.

- Project a large-scale image of the experience in the atelier near the indoor easels and paint carts.
- Offer choices of large and small easels or painting flat at the table while in the field.
- Cut or tear the easel paintings and use the pieces for a large-scale collage composition.

Infant Microgestures and Color

As a pallet for the day's work, the teachers chose a large light box and an acrylic tray of colored sand designs in hues of yellow and green. This light table, with an equally large clear tray used for creating and manipulating sand designs in the color lab, often serves as a transformative canvas of shape, color, and texture. Each morning, the children are greeted by a new creation atop the gritty canvas. The ever-changing designs create a playful game of anticipation and wonder. This morning, the sandscape of green and yellow resembled the vivid yellow flowers that had bloomed across campus. The children were invited to explore the properties of light, sand, color, and movement as they moved their hands and feet across the sand. We wondered how the use of light might further transform the shades and hues of color.

How might the amount, layering, and placement of the sand affect the color? How can the children's manipulation of the sand create new color compositions?

Scooping, sprinkling, and swiping, the children explored the texture and movement of this open-ended material, creating new hues, shades, and pigments. As they moved the colored sand about, their microgestures left behind trails and traces of their experimentation. This game of covering and uncovering, in combination with light, offered an opportunity to build an enhanced understanding of color, texture, line, and light in new ways.

Big Ideas and Concepts:

- Color
- Light
- Texture
- Transformation
- Composition
- Movement
- Color mixing
- Gradation
- Opacity
- Permanent vs. impermanent

Teachers' Thoughts and Wonderings:

- The children manipulated the sand as if looking to see what was beneath it.
- The children used small and broad gestures to create a new sandscape atop the light table.
- It appeared as though the children connected their movements with the movement of the sand.

Possible Next Steps:

- Create an immersive sandscape that includes projected images of the yellow flower field and a large-scale "canvas" that the children could manipulate with their whole bodies.
- Add natural materials to the sandscape to encourage the children to create their own sand compositions.

Nature continues to be an inexhaustible resource in our context. Both children and teachers gain inspiration from being in the outdoors, as the natural world offers authentic avenues for exploring color, smell, shadow, opacity, gravity, texture, and more. The combination of atelier materials and nature adds a layer of complexity to the experience.

We encourage you to find places that encourage exploration of the natural world and to invite children to manipulate and discover the affordances of natural materials on their own. Invite them to combine their investigations with artistic mediums, and both inside and outside, as these experiences will not only bring great joy to you and the children you work with but will also offer opportunities for deep and meaningful learning.

Chapter 7: A Celebration of Season

The Delicate Nature of Summer

As this school year began, we noticed that children found serenity in nature as we walked around campus. We wondered how the infant patio might support the children's transition to school and their budding relationships within the classroom.

- How might planters filled with carefully selected plants of various textures, shades, and hues provide opportunities for investigation and exploration?
- How could the invitation on the patio space be made a social encounter?
- How would the children begin to reveal their personalities through the unique strategies they employed to approach the invitation?

Small groups of infants were seated in Bumbo chairs within reach of the patio planters and plants within them. Teachers placed themselves intentionally in the action, taking a moment to acknowledge that children were being invited to touch and interact with elements that adults often censor or tightly regulate. The teachers offered the children time and quiet as they began their investigation. Watching carefully for "thinking feet"—toes curled and feet either very active or very still—the teachers gently offered questions or observations to the children in response to the children's gestures and microgestures. The children, seemingly mesmerized by the height, textures, and smells of the experiences, began reaching for items of interest. Responding to the serenity and gentleness of the moment, the children handled the plants delicately, seeming to appreciate them as a sort of treasure as they picked small pieces of the plant or slowly and softly rubbed the leaves or petals between their tiny fingers and toes. At times, the children referenced their teachers as if to ask, "Can I continue? Are these all for me?" Encouraged by the smiles and reassurance of their teachers, they daintily navigated the fragile materials while uncovering the many layers that nature's complexity offered, such as texture, color, smell, temperature, size, pliability, transformation, height, and delicate vs. durable. This encounter left teachers wondering how they could build upon these explorations with differing textures, scents, sizes, temperatures, and colors of natural materials.

Big Ideas and Concepts:

- Relationship
- Texture
- Delicate
- Serenity
- Shared experience
- Treasure
- Collective inquiry
- Growth
- Plants
- Size
- Flowers
- Sense of place
- Sense of belonging
- Strategy
- Appreciation
- Quiet moment
- Gestures and microgestures
- Scent
- Sense of security
- Trust
- Temperature
- Color
- Proximity
- Dainty

Teachers' Thoughts and Wonderings:

- The children found encouragement by being together.
- They confidently reached for the unknown textures before them.
- There were quiet pauses and bodies were still through their first encounters.
- As the encounter wore on, the thinking feet and gestures of children became more active.
- The children referenced their teachers for encouragement.
- The children appeared to find solace in the outdoor environment.
- The children offered their discoveries to their new friends sitting beside them.

Possible Next Steps:

- Explore the juxtaposition between delicate and sturdy and smooth vs. textured.
- Explore decomposition.
- Add plants of various scents, colors, and textures.
- Immerse the children in plants that are tall. Take a trip to the field?

The Smooth Hardness of Stone

Wondering what a juxtaposition of texture, temperature, weight, hardness, and density could offer in relation to the delicate nature of the planter of flowers and herbs, the teachers created an occasion with a composition of mounding rocks. Would the children inherently know the difference? Would they use different strategies to approach this material than they did the delicate plants? How would they rely on their friends for support? In what ways would they look to their teachers for encouragement and reassurance?

Understanding that learning is co-constructed and social, the teachers intentionally placed the infants next to each other or in a circle. Undeterred by the vast difference between the previous materials and the rocks, the children's strategies ranged from the familiar grasping and scraping to fully wrapping their hands around the smooth surfaces and lifting the weight in the air. As they became more familiar with the characteristics of the materials, they were bolder in their actions, lifting the rocks to their mouths or dropping them on the rug or upon other rocks. We wondered if the children were surprised by the sounds the rocks made and their ability to make them. Fascinated by the ways in which the children approached the challenge of weight and movement, the teachers wondered how many ways they could offer further experimentation with weight and movement and what other concepts might emerge.

Big Ideas and Concepts:

- Density
- Weight
- Texture
- Shape
- Pattern
- Sound
- Relationship
- Nature
- Contrast
- Comparison
- Determination

Teachers' Thoughts and Wonderings:

- The children were not deterred by the difference in weight of the rocks vs. the weight of the previous materials they had worked with.
- They appeared to observe one another as they built strategies for manipulating the rocks.
- How could we offer the same materials to the children in a way that would encourage stacking?

Possible Next Steps:

- Offer the heavy stones alongside more delicate natural materials to invite the children to explore the similarities and differences.
- Visit the boulder scramble on campus to encourage big movement.
- Create interesting compositions to welcome the children onto the patio.
- Revisit the concept of delicate and introduce decomposition, perhaps with fall leaves.

An Autumn Occasion

Nature seemed to anticipate our next encounter as the leaves began their first flutters toward the ground. Could a venture beyond the playground offer an immersive experience in the spritely movements, airy weight, crisp textures, and musty smells of early fall leaves? Again, positioning the children alongside their friends and offering time and space for quiet research, the teachers watched for ways the vastness of the space and the abundance of fallen leaves beckoned children's strategies for discovery. While some children used delicate gestures, others embraced the opportunity for a full-body experience. Some seemed to still completely at the sound of the crackling leaves and the wind, while others were eager to join in manipulating the leaves. Some appeared to be taking in a macroperspective, watching the branches move in the wind as the leaves danced toward the ground. Other children seemingly embraced the microperspective by honing in on the details of a single leaf. All appeared to be fascinated by the leaves' movements and the ways they changed based on the wind, the weight of the leaf, and the position in which they landed. A leaf that landed in a puddle was particularly intriguing as it shifted the movements of the leaf and the water completely.

Big Ideas and Concepts:

- Fallen leaves vs. leaves on the trees
- Weight
- Crunch
- Texture
- Smells
- Transformation
- Sound
- Vastness
- Height
- Movement
- Full-body exploration
- Social gathering
- Macro- and microperspectives
- Stillness
- Effects of wind
- Trees
- Descent of the leaf
- Puddle
- Movement of water

Teachers' Thoughts and Wonderings:

- The children were particularly intrigued by the effects of a falling leaf on a puddle of water.
- Children were content to cover themselves in leaves as they explored the sounds of crunching.
- Some focused on the leaves falling around them, while others focused on the leaves on the ground.
- The lack of weight seemed to intrigue them.
- Some picked up individual leaves, while others picked up armfuls.

Possible Next Steps:

- Explore combinations of leaves, water, and movement.
- Create an experience using both fresh green leaves and dried brown leaves, perhaps in the immersive studio.
- Ask families to take walks in their neighborhoods and collect a variety of leaves.

Falling Leaves in Water—A Digital Immersive Encounter

Noticing the infants' fascination with leaves and movement, we wondered how many other ways we could explore this. Could the immersive studio, made of mirrors bent in IMAX fashion and located under a loft, provide interesting possibilities? We curated familiar fallen branches of leaves and placed those in the studio, along with an overhead projector. We added a clear acrylic box with water, leaves, and a water pump inside; a projected video of leaves floating down the creek that the children had witnessed on their walks; the sound of leaves rustling in a light fall wind; and leaves they had gathered from their walk sprinkled on the mirrored floor. This microenvironment seemed magical to the children, and they were enticed to add leaves, experiment with motion, and orient anew to the sights and sounds of a fall transformation. Light, color, shadow, movement, size, embedded technology, color, and sound captivated the children. They appeared mesmerized by the varied motions of the leaves, the sounds of the bubbling water, the whispers of the wind, and the magic of the tangible materials vs. the intangible. Undeterred by the complexity of the situation, the children immediately engaged, thinking tongues and toes in full force, as they manipulated the leaves, splashed lightly in the water, and tried to uncover the mysteries of the wind. In fact, of the many fascinations that day, the children seemed to pause at the sounds of wind as if to ask, "What is this all about?" We wondered if that might be our next step in uncovering the movements of the changing seasons. What about wind was so fascinating to the children? How could we reproduce a fall breeze? How could we embed technology in a way that enriched meaning and context?

Big Ideas and Concepts:

- Motion
- Water
- Projection
- Immersive reflection
- Transformation
- Refraction
- Sounds
- Breeze
- Magic
- Perspective
- Echoes of reality
- Tangible and intangible
- Light
- Color
- Shadow
- Size
- Embedded technology

Teachers' Thoughts and Wonderings:

- The occasion was complex, but the children were undeterred and immediately engaged.
- Some were drawn to the leaves swirling in the water. Others were drawn to the large-scale projection, and still others were drawn to the light source.
- Several children searched for the magic that was responsible for the experience.
- The breeze and sound effects added authenticity.
- Children noticed the vibrant reds, yellows, greens, and oranges.
- Some children tried to grasp the projected leaves that floated by.
- A couple of children moved to the bin of swirling leaves and dipped their hands in the water.

Possible Next Steps:

- Go on a puddle hunt with baskets of leaves.
- Create an installation that focuses on leaves in motion in wind vs. leaves in motion in water.
- Add studio materials of autumn colors alongside fall leaves.
- Project images of the woods where the children have taken walks.

An Autumn Palette of Wind, Movement, and Color

In hopes of somehow capturing the mysteries of an autumn day, we digitally projected a familiar image of the shades of fall (taken when the children were walking on campus) onto a white pallet. Next, we layered swaths of fabric and yarn balls in hues of autumn, as well as leaves of various sizes and shapes that the children had gathered on walks. We placed a wind tunnel nearby.

The infants reacted with outstretched hands, thinking toes, and animated gestures. They were happily surprised by the first swirling leaf and remained transfixed as they quietly stared at the spot where it came from. They were intermittently overactive and still. They joyfully shrieked in astonishment as more leaves sailed through the air and floated across the fabric. Reaching to capture some and giggling as others moved past, the children remained enamored by the whirling dance of the leaves. The subtle motion from the video projected on the pallet added another curious element. Which leaves could be grasped, and which remained elusive? As we observed and documented, we wondered: In what other ways could we explore the sensory experiences of changing seasons?

Big Ideas and Concepts:

- Wind
- Movement
- Projection
- Texture
- Conversation
- Scale
- Size
- Shape
- Memory
- Revisiting
- Fluidity of fabric
- Fall colors
- Swirling
- Launch
- Descent
- Float
- Tumble
- Whirl
- Tangible and intangible

Teachers' Thoughts and Wonderings:

- The children's surprise in the whirling, launched leaves was evident.
- The children were intermittently overactive and still.
- There were joyful shrieks in response to the unexpected.
- The children seemed to recognize the familiar image projected in the space.
- They appeared to participate in a game of waiting for the next moving leaf to approach.

Possible Next Steps:

- Add more fall elements from nature.
- Explore the scents of fall.
- Add new textures.
- Create more immersive tangible experiences, such as cooking.

A Simmering Pot

We wondered if the addition of autumn smells would add a layer of interest to the invitation. We surveyed the families of the infants to learn what smells evoked thoughts and feelings of the fall season. With those results as our guide, the teachers collected cranberries, apples, cinnamon sticks, lemons, thyme, cloves, and oranges to create a simmering pot.

The children gently placed the fragrant ingredients into the pot, tasting several along the way. While our original thinking centered around the smells of this experience, the children clearly had other ideas. They tasted, squished, and smelled, creating a full sensory exploration. Over several days, the children were enchanted as the ingredients transformed before their eyes.

While the pot simmered and the scents filled the room, the educators wondered how the addition of scent might further inspire the infants' curiosity. Does scent trigger memories for the children? How do scent, taste, and touch combine to provoke memories and feelings and create a sense of community? How do the aromas reflect the cultures and traditions of the infants and their families?

Big Ideas and Concepts:

- Fragrance
- Texture
- Transformation
- Taste
- Scent
- Color
- Diffusion
- Combination

- Stirring
- The joy of being together
- Social exchange
- Weight
- Size
- Tactile
- Composition
- Tradition
- Community
- Sour
- Sweet

Teachers' Thoughts and Wonderings:

- The children were intentional in placing their chosen ingredients into the pot.
- Taste was particularly alive this day.
- The children squished, crushed, and smooshed in ways we had not seen them do before.
- Their engagement remained over several days.
- The children were fascinated by the different presentations of an orange.
- Cinnamon was a particular favorite, and the children seemed to be drawn to the movement of the cranberries in the water.

Possible Next Steps:

- Find additional ways to connect memories and scent, and family and scent.
- Find ways to include scent in more experiences.
- As the season is changing, find ways to explore the change in temperature.

Colors, Textures, and Temperature of Winter

As the temperatures chilled and frost developed across windowpanes, we wondered how we might summon the winter season to play. Curating an experience with various ice forms, cold water, and the cool hues of ice blue and white, we invited the children to uncover cold. A background window offered reciprocity between the outdoor sights of winter and white and blue ribbons hanging from the ceiling. The sounds of crackling ice played softly in the background as the children approached the invitation. They drew near with fascination as they dunked their hands in a bucket of blue-tinted water and ice, attempted to lift a slippery ice mass from a bowl, and appeared to analyze the color, shape, and density of ice pops. Perplexed yet unfazed by cold hands, they remained engaged and committed to their research as they looked to one another for reinforcement and validation. As the children worked, the teachers wondered how many strategies the children would create to move the elusive ice forms. Did the children make connections between their cold hands due to the materials and their cold hands when outside? Did they notice the presentation of different ice forms? Did they interpret them all as ice? What were they thinking in the long moments they gazed at the ice popsicles they held?

Big Ideas and Concepts:

- Frost
- Cold
- Ice
- Water
- Blue
- Transformation
- Sturdy
- Slippery
- Melt
- Freeze
- Permanence vs. impermanence
- Density
- Circularity

Teachers' Thoughts and Wonderings:

- The children were undeterred by the temperature of the ice, but the melting was perplexing.
- They made connections between the different shapes and textures of the ice, while recognizing both were ice.
- The ice pops allowed time for children to observe ice melting and to know cold through taste.
- The slippery nature of the ice cubes created a conundrum.

Possible Next Steps:

- Consider building on the children's interests in tasting.
- Find other interesting forms to create shapes of ice in both large and small scales.
- Unpack the various sensorial experiences of winter.

Smells, Colors, and Textures from the Holiday Kitchen

Inspired by cooking and other beautiful moments of the winter holiday season, we envisioned an experience that would hold those scents, textures, sights, sounds, and warmth. Again turning to our families as resources for inspiration, we invited their participation in gathering and collecting materials that reflected the cultures and traditions of each child's family. We created a scene with small fir trees, rope lights, boughs of evergreens, baking ingredients, and small smelling bottles and sachets filled with cloves, cinnamon, and nutmeg. We mixed scented dough that we rolled and placed in muffin tins and rolled out on cutting boards.

The children manipulated the various materials as they moved dough from one tin compartment to the next, shook globes of water and cranberries, and pinched and poked dough as if testing its elasticity and permanency. Seemingly transfixed by the dough's ability to transform, the children smashed it and delighted in their discovery of how to make it flat. As the children explored, we wondered how many ways we might enhance the reciprocity between home and school through experiences. In what ways does the complexity of the invitation increase the complexity of the children's thinking and learning? How does the transformative property of the dough deepen the children's understanding of the material? How many other materials could we add that mirror the holiday experience?

Big Ideas and Concepts:

- Scent
- Texture
- Sound
- Taste
- Color
- Warmth (temperature)
- Warmth as a feeling
- Family tradition
- Communication
- Cultural tradition
- Baking
- Fragrance
- Compartment
- Transformation
- Movement
- Dough
- Elasticity
- Malleability
- Complexity

Teachers' Thoughts and Wonderings:

- Teachers noticed that the children were drawn to strong scents.
- The affordance of transformation that the dough provided was particularly intriguing to the children.
- The cranberry globes in combination with the light were fascinating.
- Children showed preferences for particular scented bottles.

Possible Next Steps:

- Explore how the holiday season affords possibilities for connecting with families.
- Revisit and relaunch cold and winter invitations.
- Find other ways to bring in families' cultures and traditions.
- Create an immersive studio with icebergs and large chunks of ice.
- Investigate the absence of color and winter.
- Create experiences that combine winter and other materials from the atelier.
- Explore snow.
- Follow the flight path of a snowflake.
- Explore the weight of ice compared to the weight of a snowflake.
- Further unpack the thawing process, perhaps by exploring mud.

The Essence of Spring

Having fully explored the essence of winter, and noting hints of spring, we transitioned to possibilities this season held. The blooming flowers and warmer temperatures returned, inspiring us to bring the joy and nuance of the season into our classroom. The infants could now sit up independently, so we decided to change the perspective of the invitation to reflect the shift in the children's perspective. The educators wondered how an aerial installation filled with spring flowers could offer a different view of the flowers. The children were intrigued by the intricate details found on the petals and leaves as they reached and pulled to try to get a closer look at each bundle. Gently rubbing the petals, they seemed to notice the difference in textures between the fresh flowers and the ice of the previously encountered winter material. As the children gazed between the pink, purple, and yellow petals, they seemed to be taking note of the differences in hue and shade, building a catalog of colors that is much richer than the colors found in a crayon box.

Noticing the children's desire to push and pull the flowers, the educators wondered how the addition of wind would affect the experience. Would the children recognize this familiar material when presented in an unfamiliar way? How else might we deepen the relationship between the children and color?

Big Ideas and Concepts:

- Perspective
- Details
- Texture
- Color
- Vibrant
- Delicate
- Prickly
- Dimensionality
- Contrast between the fresh soft and the hard cold
- Scent
- Complexity of a flower
- Decomposition
- Growth
- Return of color
- Length

Teachers' Thoughts and Wonderings:

- The children naturally shifted their movements to delicate and nuanced gestures.
- They attempted to test the various textures by rolling them in their fingers.
- A few children seemed mesmerized.
- The addition of an arial invitation offered an interesting, mild disorientation.
- The bright colors seemed to draw the children in.

Possible Next Steps:

- Add wind.
- Add light and the invitation to shadow.
- Layer the floor with similar flowers so that they were both above and below the children.
- Include vases of tall flowers sitting on the floor.
- Combine the immersive studio with a wide variety of colorful flowers of different sizes and textures.

Celebrating the magic and mystery of changing seasons, teachers offered a variety of multisensory, curated occasions for discovery. Invited into complex situations where texture, color, temperature, light, smells, wind, water, digital landscapes, and overhead projection fuse together, the children found themselves immersed in autumn's color transformations, winter's chill, the smells of a simmering pot, the consistencies of holiday baking, and the shades and textures of budding spring. Through a variety of complex natural palettes full of interesting and intelligent materials, children uncovered the surprises and complexity of the seasons as they moved with the intricate juxtaposition of delicate and hardy, cozy and cold, crunchy and pliable.

HAND
DUDE

Chapter 8: Digital Environments and Echoes of Reality

At Riverfield, we are fascinated by the potential that technology holds as an integrated component of daily life. To support the development of twenty-first-century skills, we are committed to creating educational experiences that include innovative technology. We approach this action research by asking ourselves how both the digital and the tangible might serve as reciprocal and symbiotic tools for meaning making and learning. One strategy we employ is finding a myriad of ways that immersive digital experiences can add layers of complexity and possibility to daily encounters. We have created immersive playscapes that invite children to move beyond the boundaries of here and now, tangible and intangible, and concrete and illusive. We strive to envision and design environments where the children's interaction within the digital and physical are so interconnected it is hard to know where one ends and the other begins. Ultimately, these spaces create a duality of place, a world where children and adults ponder: Is it real? Is it here? How? From where? How do I manipulate or transform it? Can I create my own?

This chapter shares the stories of young children as researchers and digital citizens, who inherently question and discover this frontier of shifting landscapes. The stories are alive and dynamic, where children and teachers make palpable the joy of learning side by side. As our research unfolds, we find that children question, observe, test theories, rethink, relaunch, innovate, design, and create. Fully embracing the unfolding invitation to explore, it appears that the children also welcome the dance between creativity and scientific inquiry as they continually research, celebrate, articulate, and represent the tension between these dualities. In this digital world, web cams, digital microscopes, digital drawing, and immersive projection are tools with which to experiment, observe, interpret, and represent unfolding understanding.

Whispers of Light

The disco ball's gleaming exterior sends rays of light ricocheting in all directions, painting the room in a tapestry of sliced light. The space fills with an air of inquiry as the children swipe at the fragments of mirrored illumination in an attempt to capture them. The light seems both real and unreal in the same moment, offering surprise, unpredictability, and invitation for contemplation. As they interact with the light, we wonder whether the children are considering questions such as: What is the magic behind this phenomenon? What makes them appear and disappear? Can they be captured or redirected? The children's energy is contagious, and we are compelled to think further about how we can layer the tangible and intangible throughout the school environment in meaningful and relevant ways.

Big Ideas and Concepts:

- Magic
- Interplay of light, reflection, and motion
- Black/darkness
- Slices of light in the darkness
- Constellations of light
- Elusive
- Illusion
- Tangible and intangible
- Light in motion
- Minutiae
- Capture
- Evade
- Weightless
- Unpredictability
- Sources of reflection
- Shared experience
- Collective inquiry
- Joy of being together

Teachers' Thoughts and Wonderings:

- The children immediately created a joyful game of trying to capture the elusive and erratic rays of light.
- Some children moved to their stomachs to get closer to the specks of light in an attempt to capture it in their hands.
- A few children identified the disco ball as the source of the magic.
- One or two children attempted to escape the ricocheting light bursts.
- The children relied on each other for additional strategies and encouragement to figure out the mystery.

Possible Next Steps:

- Add a collection of small disco balls so children can capture the light and bounce it throughout the room through their own movements.
- Add reflective spheres to move light as they roll through the room.
- Add large mylar balloons filled with helium to capture and move light in interesting ways as the children bounce the balloons through the space.
- Intermittently cover and uncover the light source to make light constellations disappear and reappear.

An Intangible Peacock Muse

The children's relationships with the freely wandering peacocks on our campus offer endless inspiration and possibility. For these experiences, we projected an image taken by one of the children against a backdrop of mounded blocks of clay. The room is aglow with the soft, mesmerizing hues of a digital peacock, its feathers a hypnotic symphony of color and patterns. As the children navigate the mound of clay blocks, they explore the height, density, sturdiness, weight, and multidimensionality afforded. The teachers are aware of the calculated risk but embrace the role that risk plays in constructing knowledge and remain committed to the possibilities for adventure and learning.

Over time, large full-body movements give way to smaller gestures. The children begin digging fingers and tools into the malleable surfaces. The clay yields to their actions, taking shape under their small hands. This medium, pliable and earthy, contrasts intriguingly with the futuristic projection that surrounds them. Their fingers explore the clay's texture, feeling its coolness and pliancy, grounding them in the physicality of their art. It is a beautiful harmony of the analog and digital worlds. The digital projection of the peacock offers a magical canvas for the children's creativity. With each deft movement of their hands, the children transform the clay with their intricate marks, mirroring the delicate patterns of the peacock's feathers. The connection between the physical and digital realms is seamless, as if the clay itself is a bridge between two dimensions. As the children work, they remain in tune with the shifting tableau of the peacock. The children draw inspiration from their peacock muse, its regal poise, and the kaleidoscope of colors that adorn its plumage.

Big Ideas and Concepts:

- Clay
- Digital landscape
- Malleability
- Scale
- Density
- Weight
- Height
- Full-body experience
- Projection
- Color
- Big
- Hues
- Relationship
- Pattern
- Multidimensionality
- Sturdiness
- Conversation
- Perspective
- Tangible and intangible

Teachers' Thoughts and Wonderings:

- The children seemed unfazed by the invitation to climb.
- They took calculated risks when climbing to gain a different perspective.
- The children seemed to rely on their friends for support when navigating the clay blocks.
- Some children chose to stay firmly planted on the ground and observed the projection both on the walls and on the clay.
- The children were mesmerized by the details of the feather magnified before them.
- The children seemed to use the projection as a "map" to create line and shape.

Possible Next Steps:

- Add clay coils and balls to encourage composition.
- Add a variety of materials—collage, paint, wire, textiles, mark-making tools—to represent the essence of the peacock feathers.
- Offer small clay slabs to see how children translate the line and shape of the feather.

Neon-Tape Sculptures

After observing the children's penchant for the mysteries of tape in the classroom over many days, we wondered how we might design invitations that layered complex experiences in imaginative ways. How might we invite the children to sculpt? How many ways can we use tape to play with the power of line? How could we draw attention to color? We began with an installation that included large, donated PVC pipe tubes set upright in a transformable black-box space. We added several rolls of neon tape, neon plastic wire, black lights, and a colorful geometric projection. We offered the space with little explanation and watched as the children unraveled, wadded, stretched, draped, stuck, and unstuck the materials around the room—fashioning a multidimensional tribute to stickiness, line, and color. We were fascinated by the strategies the children employed. They relied on each other to collaboratively navigate the inherent challenges of unrolling and adhering a flexible medium.

Amid the focused work, the children appeared to be playing a game of line, competing to see what lines stretched farthest, sagged the most, or zigzagged more elaborately. In an attempt to deepen the children's research, we offered an iPad and a digital drawing app. The children responded immediately with an innate sense of how to use the tool. A symphony of colorful lines, created on and projected from the tablet, darted across the room mirroring the bold lines of the meticulously placed tape. Disrupted on occasion by the towers of PVC pipe, the lines bent and twisted around the children's ode to tape, creating a digital reality that echoed the reality fabricated through tangible materials. We were fascinated and wondered whether a projected kaleidoscope might offer additional inspiration for creative license with line and color. Could projections of architectural elements add simulated detail to the sculpture?

Big Ideas and Concepts:

- Sticky
- Vibrancy
- Color
- Transformation of color
- Sculpture
- Height
- Length
- Dimension
- Projection
- Reflection
- Form
- Experimenting
- Digital mark making
- Line
- Combination
- Multimedia
- Collaboration
- Glow

Teachers' Thoughts and Wonderings:

- The children were drawn to the seemingly never-ending rolls of tape.
- The children stretched the tape pieces to connect the PVC tubes.
- They were intrigued to discover what tape did and did not stick to.
- They worked together to unroll and re-roll the tape spools.
- Their digital marks mirrored the tape sculpture they created.

Possible Next Steps:

- Project the digital marks around the black room as inspiration for continued sculpture.
- Offer small stepladders so the children can add tape above them.
- Offer tape in different forms—balls, rolled pieces, different lengths—to add dimensionality to the sculpture.

A Game of Hide-and-Seek

Building on the children's interest in color and the teacher's awareness of the vivid hues of a coral reef, the educators wondered how an immersive experience in a digital underwater landscape could support the children's emerging theories around these concepts. When the children entered the space, they were surprised to find it transformed. Hanging papers, translucent fabrics, and mounds of white batting provided surfaces where the fish, moving back and forth, fast and slow, darted and disappeared as they swam. Curious about where the fish were going, the children began searching for them, creating a game of hide-and-seek along the way. The children hid behind the paper sheets and peered around the sides of the paper. Repeatedly, they tried to capture the fish as they swam by. The children, fascinated by the elusive nature of the fish and entertained by the hunt for or escape from their friends, happily engaged in a game of hide-and-seek that bridged the real and unreal.

Big Ideas and Concepts:

- Game
- Hide-and-seek
- Appear and disappear
- Scale
- Motion through water
- Coral reef
- Dimensionality (floor to ceiling)
- Speed
- Capture
- Escape
- Present
- Elusive
- Real
- Unreal

Teachers' Thoughts and Wonderings:

- The children seemed inspired by the fish to play hide-and-seek.
- At first they are hiding from the fish, but then begin hiding from and seeking each other.
- The children begin to use boxes as an attempt to capture the elusive fish in the digital landscape.
- Some of the children began telling simple stories regarding the fish and their attempts to escape.

Possible Next Steps:

- Add other ways to play hide-and-seek.
- Add large mounds of white tulle to create additional illusions and "hiding spots" for the fish.
- Add tangible fish shapes inside some of the boxes.
- Create holes in some of the strips of paper.
- Add long strips of translucent paper.
- Add white construction materials to provide dimensionality coming up from the floor.

Kaleidoscopes of Color

For this experience, the educators wondered how they might entice the children to more deeply explore the classroom environment. Could the addition of light and projection encourage the children to explore previously neglected areas? The teachers intentionally curated a series of provocations in their light-and-reflection area in the classroom and observed as the children were drawn to the colors swirling and reflecting from the mirrored surfaces. Some of the children manipulated the lights, and others were more interested in seeing their reflections. Noticing one child off to the side, the teacher stopped to observe as the child sat quietly for several minutes. The child's eyes followed the motion of the projection, and the teacher noticed that she began moving the papers beneath her. It appeared that she was trying to capture and move the lights and reflections below her. She followed the projection with pieces of white paper, chasing the sparkles until she was positioned in a way that the reflections and projections appeared on her paper. Excited at her discovery, she gleefully shared her findings with her peers and educators. Propelled by her curiosity, the teachers wondered how to offer further opportunities for the children to move and capture light. Would the children be as interested in moving and capturing natural light as they were the projected light? How does the presentation of materials affect the children's interest in and participation with areas of the environment?

Big Ideas and Concepts:

- Light
- Kaleidoscope
- Reflection
- Transformation of light
- Movement
- Projection
- Tangible vs. intangible
- Color
- Immersive

Teachers' Thoughts and Wonderings:

- Children were drawn to capturing light on paper.
- The children seemingly question how the projection is captured and how it moved across the papers and mirrors.
- Children began moving paper and large materials to "capture" the light and projections.

Possible Next Steps:

- Develop our own kaleidoscope to manipulate and move colors.
- Add sheer, colored textiles, such as fabrics, vinyl, and transparencies.
- Add materials to construct a kaleidoscope.

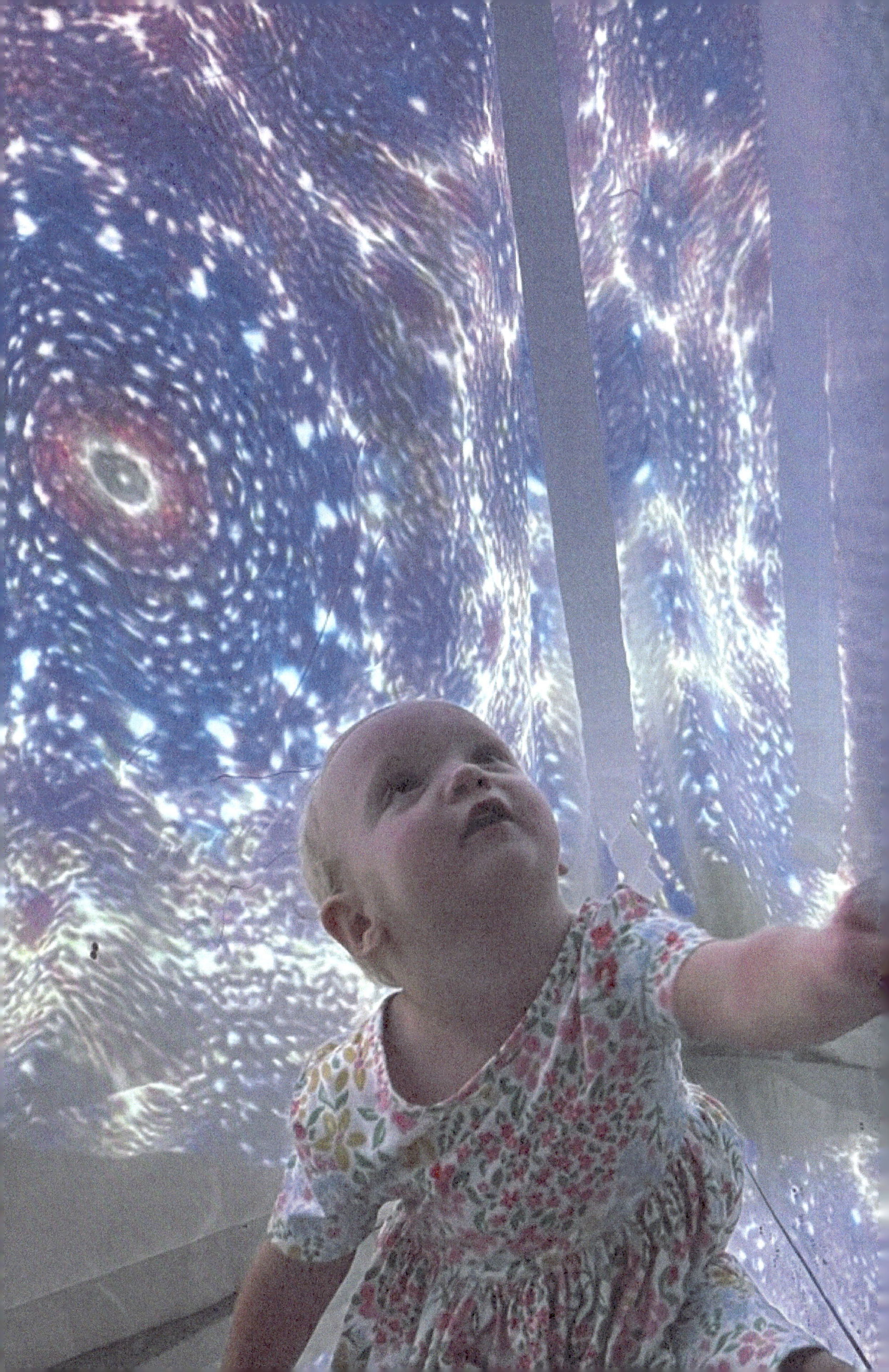

Autumn Augmented Reality

Pouncing on an opportunity to transform a vacant space into an immersive studio, the educators worked collaboratively to create an environment resembling a virtual-reality experience. They added floor-to-ceiling projection and strategically placed mirrors that reflected the projections above and below the children. Tactile materials offered a layer of "real" to an otherwise digital environment. Drawing inspiration from the numerous walks around campus and in the woods, the teachers projected an image of a crisp, fall day into the space. Real leaves gathered by the children were sprinkled throughout, and recorded sounds of leaves crunching and crackling played overhead. A nearby wind tunnel and baskets of leaves offered opportunities for launching and coaxed the children to re-create a windy autumn day.

Small easels, along with paints mixed by the children in the fiery hues of fall, enticed them to make marks representative of the changing season. Awestruck as they entered, the children moved gingerly through this new and magical space. First taking time to survey the scene, some children joyfully approached the paint, eager to leave their marks on the easels. Working both independently and in tandem, the children filled the canvases with their interpretations of fall. Other children worked with the wind tunnel, setting afloat piles of leaves and watching as they spiraled and scattered to the ground. The variety of experiences offered within the studio gave the children opportunities to engage as both observers and participants. They shared spaces, offered strategies, and lent support to each other, reminding us of the roles that environment and materials play in the development and curation of experiences. As the educators observed the deep and meaningful encounter, they wondered what other digital landscapes could provide context for the space. What other areas of campus could we project? How can we continue to offer experiences that alter perspective, embrace all the senses, and encourage interaction with materials?

Toddler Encounters with a Medley of Dimensionality and Color

After observing the toddlers' interest in paint, nature, and collage as they navigated their classroom, these teachers wondered how their classroom environment might further support the children's budding interests. Could an immersive studio space filled with the projection of a field of fall flowers and bouquets of real flowers and stocked with collage and paint materials lend support to the children? Beginning with large-scale collage, as this was a familiar medium to the children, the educators offered various sizes and textures of the hues found in the projected field. They presented the papers in a variety of ways as well, some in crumpled bits, some folded into accordions, and some in flat pieces of different shapes, to invite the children to represent the display before them. Accepting the challenge, the children quickly set to work arranging the materials on the canvas with intentionality, precision, and joy. As they worked, they continually looked to their friends and educators, inviting questions, feedback, and suggestions. The children's proud, smiling faces and happy dances made their confidence that their efforts had produced an interpretative representation of the images surrounding them visible. They proudly walked their compositions through their friends' classrooms and waited with anticipation to share their work with their families.

Returning to the previous projection for continued inspiration, the educators wondered how a paint experience might build on the children's inquiry around color, flowers, and expression. With vivid hues of red, orange, yellow, and pink, the educators invited the children to experiment with paint mixing. From small bottles lining the edges of the studio space, the children gently poured out dollops of color to create their own unique shades. They watched in amazement as they stirred and mixed the colors together, creating new and unexpected surprises. Armed with their newly mixed paints, the children returned to the studio space several days later to begin painting. With the projection around and below them, the children began adding their strokes and brush marks to the canvases on the floor and on the easels next to them. They shrieked and squealed as they made marks that imitated the petals of the flowers. Referencing both the projected flowers and the real flowers before them, the children seemed delighted in their interpretations. As the teachers observed and documented, they wondered how the size and scale of a collage or painting might alter the children's perspective. How many other ways could they represent the flowers using materials from the atelier? How does the combination of the tangible and intangible pique the children's curiosity?

Big Ideas and Concepts:

- Color spectrum
- Sticky
- Contrast
- Vibrancy
- Projection
- Flowers
- Scent
- Nature
- Texture
- Height
- Collage and composition
- Part to whole
- Shadow
- Dimensionality

- Scale
- Garden
- Sequence
- Deconstruction
- Augmented reality
- Perspective
- Shape
- Line
- Paint

Teachers' Thoughts and Wonderings:

- The children approached the paint and paintbrushes with confidence, choosing color with great intention.
- Some children were drawn to paint while others were drawn to collage.

Possible Next Steps:

- Create a mixed-media piece that incorporates both paint and collage of the flower projection.
- Work in small groups to create collaborative paintings on small canvases.
- Create a large-scale painting with cool hues created by the children.
- Incorporate wire into the flower representations.
- Work with the children on the curation of a mixed-media piece using the collage and painted works.

The Natural Atelier: Transformation

At the start of a new year, the educators of this toddler class were intrigued by the possibilities of a natural atelier and how to harness the unique affordances of nature to spark curiosity, wonder, and joy. After educators observed the children in the classroom, it became apparent that the children also were interested in the possibilities this space held.

The next day, the children were greeted by a space adorned with flowers in colors of the rainbow, mortars and pestles, sifters, scissors, glue, and small wooden pallets for display. Eager to begin the work, the children set out grinding, mashing, stirring, sifting, and mixing the natural materials. The transformation that was happening before their very eyes was intriguing and perplexing. The children seemed interested in creating a gradation of size with each material and sharing their findings with each other and their teachers.

Eyeing the pallets laying on the table, the children turned their attention to the creation of collage. As they worked, teachers observed and documented the strategies children employed as they grappled with mathematical concepts such as color, symmetry, proportion, pattern, scale, size, and shape. While some children chose the size and shape of the flower petals based on the size and shape of the pallet they were gluing on, others paid careful attention to the colors of the petals. Some children were careful to group like textures together. Others created simple patterns with stems and petals, intentionally placing each piece. Some heaped bits and pieces in mounds, and others focused on filling the entire space. No matter the strategy applied, with each dab of glue and placement of the tiny treasures, the children's vision for the collective composition came to life.

Building on the experience, the educators wondered how a field of digital flowers projected atop the table in the natural atelier and combined with familiar collage materials would alter the children's interactions. How would the children react if we added mark-making tools with and without projection? Could we combine collage and graphic representation to create a multimedia piece of art? Stepping back to observe, the educators noticed the children's deep fascination with the colors of the chalk pastels and how they mimicked the colors of the flowers. Carefully choosing pastels that imitated the flowers' colors, the children gently traced the lines found in both the tangible and digital blossoms, making marks representative of the details they saw in each bloom in front of them. While some children chose to work with the mark-making materials, others turned to the familiarity of collage to represent their thinking. Skilled in the art of composition, the children gathered their treasures, placed small dabs of glue on their chosen pallets, and diligently placed each item atop the pieces of wood. Through this process, we wondered if natural collage could serve as a way to connect with and appreciate the beauty of the natural world. What stories are the children telling through their collage? What theories are the children building around the natural world and their understanding of materials used to represent it?

Big Ideas and Concepts:

- Natural world
- Transformation
- Color
- Collage
- Size
- Symmetry
- Proportion
- Shape
- Texture
- Digital landscape
- Line
- Mark making
- Multimedia

Teachers' Thoughts and Wonderings:

- The children appeared to move seamlessly between the two media offered, showing no obvious preference between collage and mark making.
- When working collaboratively, the children shared the space with respect. They worked together to add pieces to the multimedia piece but also had moments of individual work.

Possible Next Steps:

- Create a large-scale, collaborative collage representing the floral digital landscapes the children were familiar with.
- Alongside the children, curate the smaller natural collages into a classroom exhibit.

Delving into the concept of immersive experiences, or digital landscapes, where digital and physical elements intertwine to facilitate learning and meaning making, this chapter investigates the innovative and interesting ways to integrate digital technology. Through various anecdotes and examples, we highlight the dynamic interactions among children, teachers, and technology, emphasizing the role of inquiry, innovation, experimentation, and creativity in the learning process. The chapter begins with an exploration of the "Whispers of Light," in which children engage with a disco ball's reflections, prompting questions about the phenomenon and nature of reality. The chapter then moves on to discuss experiences such as projecting images of peacocks onto clay surfaces, creating neon-tape sculptures under the glow of black light, and immersing children in digital underwater landscapes, all of which highlight the illusive echoes of reality. Throughout the chapter, the narrative emphasizes the seamless integration of digital and physical elements, such as digital drawing alongside tangible materials such as markers, tape, and clay. It also highlights the role of educators in observing and facilitating children's interactions with technology, while also reflecting on the pedagogical implications of such experiences.

The chapter concludes by discussing the transformative potential of natural ateliers, where children engage with tactile materials and digital projections to create artworks inspired by nature. It raises questions about the ways in which technology can enhance children's understanding of the natural world and their creative expression.

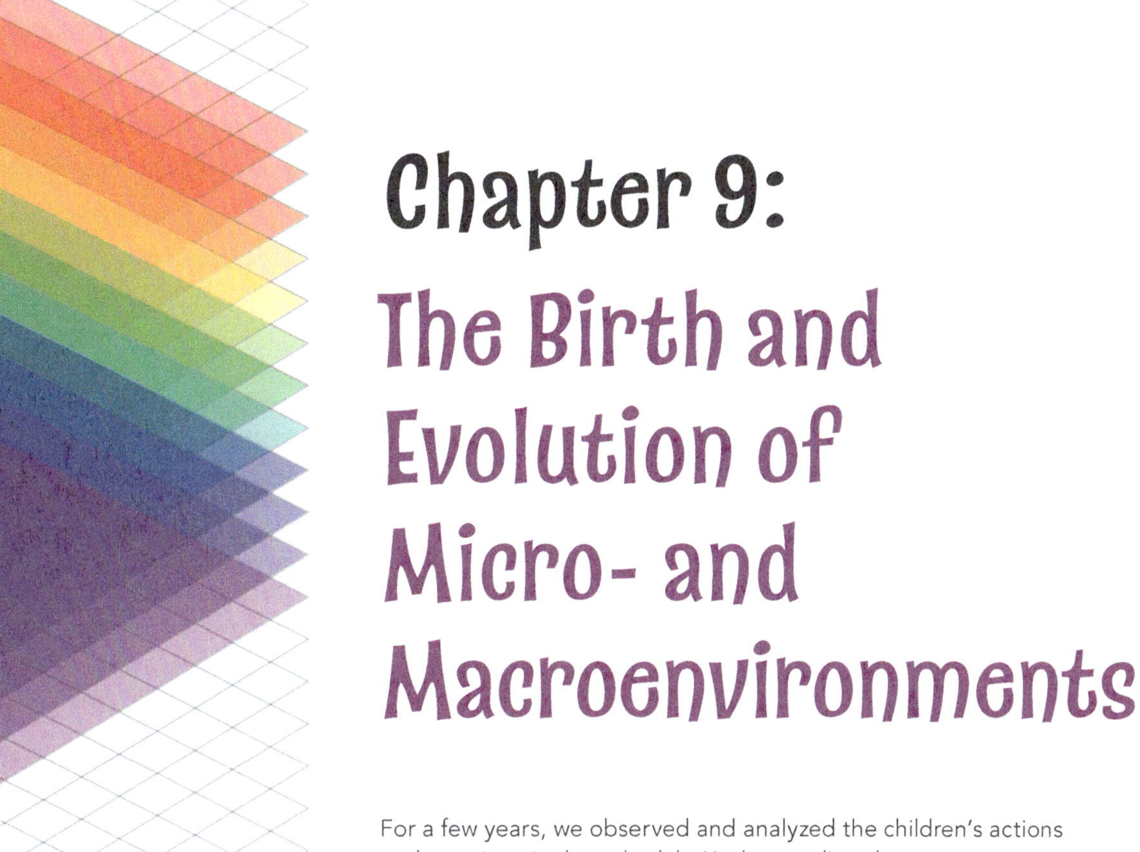

Chapter 9: The Birth and Evolution of Micro- and Macroenvironments

For a few years, we observed and analyzed the children's actions and reactions in the color lab. Understanding that spaces must evolve and morph to stay "alive," we wondered how we might alter the lab to extend the children's research in innovative ways. Light can have varying effects, so we proposed a mirror box illuminated by black light and situated in a corner of the studio that allowed for immersive experiences for our youngest children. We envisioned a space alive with neon color, a space that literally glowed as an invitation to all who walked by.

Black light and neon create a mesmerizing fusion of color and illumination; the combination invites an encounter where color takes on a new life and a magical quality. We wondered how many strategies for navigating the space we could invite. How many materials could we find to support the space? How many provocations could we design? How many paradigms might those provocations uncover? How would research in this microenvironment deepen the children's knowledge about light, color, and perspective? How might an immersive experience bring variety to the current installations within the color lab?

These questions drove our initial quest to invent, and we began making inventories of possibility. We began by analyzing documentation from prior years to more fully understand how the color lab had been used. Then, we designed the new boxed environment. The result was a hideaway that played with infinite reflection, augmented reality, and the visual riddle of black light and color.

Next, we began imagining the intelligent materials that could play inside it. How many things are available in neon? Do all neon colors glow under black light? do all shades of white? How many textures could we offer? How many shapes and sizes? We gathered papers, stirring sticks, plastic containers, tape, confetti, neon liquids, fabrics, melted neon bottles, neon lacing strings, Slinkies, balls, bubbles, and book illustrations to fill the space. With the motivation to ignite inquiry and incite adventure, we curated an invitation where the union of black light and neon created a repertoire of possibility.

The black light was transformative in more ways than we had anticipated. Observing the children in their playful encounter, we noted that the space created a passage from the ordinary to the extraordinary. The children had been fascinated by a paper studio that had recently been developed. We built on this idea as we wondered how we might combine the interests. Because the children were already familiar with paper, we predicted the material in combination with black light would focus their attention more fully on the phosphorescent glow and surreal vibrancy that ensued. With "thinking fingers," the children scratched at the corrugated cardboard, crunched the wadded paper, and flapped the neon strips as if the movement might explain what they saw. Through their actions, the children reminded us that there is beauty to be found in the convergence of the known and the mysterious. The children began gently peeling back the paper as if searching for the origin of the mysterious glow. We watched as they peeled and peeked, and we wondered how we could extend this experience further.

- Was it the peeling motion that appealed to them?
- Was it the mystery beneath the paper?
- Were they looking to make sure the reality of the mirror still existed?

We surmised that an encounter with neon tape might augment the children's research around peeling and peeking, so we began collecting a wide variety of tapes and palettes the children could explore. We carefully and intentionally displayed tapes in various sizes, orientations, and presentations.

When illuminated by black light, neon takes on a new life, a magical quality that is nothing short of spellbinding. The children's facial expressions, squeals, and body language conveyed they felt the same way as they eagerly approached the occasion. Again, the act of peeling back was pervasive. We were struck by the myriad of ways the children strategized to remove and then replace the strips of tape in various formations. We were also aware of what a social occasion it was. Children gathered in pairs and small groups to analyze and devise plans of action and to share their discoveries. Who knew that tape could be so fun and offer so many conceptual uncoverings? Why did the tape appear to change colors when moved away from black light? What made the "sticky"? Was it on both sides? Does all tape peel and stick in the same way or does the width matter? Why is it easier or harder to pull from some surfaces? Why is finding the beginning of a tape roll so tricky? How do you create a loop to pull more readily? As the children worked, we began to wonder what other everyday items we could combine with black light to offer a new perspective on the ordinary. We wondered if playground balls made in neon colors could provide the next provocation.

Knowing that complexity and aesthetics would be particularly important, we filled the mirror box with various patterned, glowing balls. The vivid pinks, purples, oranges, yellows, and blacks appeared as if they had been plucked from a dreamscape. The children were delighted and struggled to choose where to focus first. Was the mirror still beneath the balls? How did the balls gain their glowing power? Did they still move in the same way? What games did they invite? Moving seamlessly between quiet moments of still, intense focus and moments of interactive, gleeful encounter, the children navigated the enchantment of the ordinary turned extraordinary.

The year continued to unfold in such a pattern. Observations, documentation, and analysis of each intentionally designed experience informed the design of the next experience. Embracing an innovators mindset, the teachers embraced the challenge to re-create the realm of pure magic that the mirrored black-light box offered. Time after time, the invitations drew the children to become detectives, seeking surprises within the space and navigating the illusion of various materials in black light. They reminded us that there is extraordinary in the everyday and that adventure beckons through the lens of open and responsive possibility.

Experiments with Black Light and Color

Our most current installation in the color lab has been the addition of a black-light mirror box. Beginning as a teacher inquiry around how black light might affect color, educators wondered how the addition of black light might transform familiar materials and spark new discoveries and concepts. How could the duality of experiences with white light and black light add new understandings of color?

We filled the space with an assortment of neon-colored materials and observed as the children made their first encounters. We were unsure how the children would respond and wanted to rely on their interpretations and actions as we continued to develop the space. Entranced by the unexpected glow, the children deepened their research into color, shape, transformation, black light, reflection, and dimension. What was once familiar was seemingly new, and the children were enchanted and mildly disoriented by the shift. Their strategies for approaching the new space and its inherent magic were varied. While some approached the mystery with hesitation, others ran at full speed, fully embracing the new dimension that lay before them. No matter their approach, it was clear that the space was alive with potential, so we felt secure in moving forward with our venture, using the observations from these encounters as launch pads in our design.

"Pops" of Color

After many experiences devoted to exploring the effects of black light and neon using the neon box in the corner of the color lab dedicated to this purpose, the teachers wondered in what ways they could further embed sound and shape into the unfolding encounters. Covering the floor of the mirror box with large bubble wrap outlined in various shades of neon, the invitation to explore circularity, bumpy, compression, neon color, and popping sounds awaited. Seemingly enticed by the glowing hues, the children made their way into the box. Surprised by the popping sound under their knees, the children shifted to a seated position to investigate further. Their hands scattered across the bubbles, occasionally stopping to scrunch and pinch the intriguing plastic. Some seemed to choose a specific color to grab—perhaps thinking that color had something to do with the consequential pop that ensued. Others seemed to trace their fingers around the outline of the bubbles as though they were tactically researching the circular shapes. As we watched these gestures, we wondered how else we could explore circularity and color. Could hanging long strands of circular streamers offer possibility for this?

Crawling into the mirrored box, the children encountered vibrant streamers cascading infinitely in front of, above, and beneath them. Small fingers grasped the bright circles—seemingly pondering their shape, size, and pliability. The movement of the streamers, in contrast to the stationary nature of the bubble wrap experience, seemed to captivate the children's attention. Squeals of surprise and delight filled the air as children moved through the box with outstretched arms, gently chasing the elusive strands. Once a strand was captured, the children settled in for further research. With "thinking toes" curled and tongues out, their focus was intense, their engagement evident through their smiles, mutual encouragement and varied gestures and microgestures. When a strand was released, another was hunted, and so the game continued joyfully throughout the morning. We were struck by the delight that movement afforded in connection with color and shape and wondered in how many other ways we could innovatively research this concept.

With a multitude of experiences to draw on, the addition of neon Slinkies in the black-light box generated a new opportunity for discovery: the gradient movement of color. Greeted one day by a dozen Slinkies hanging inside the mirror box and several sitting on the ground, the children were at first in awe of the novelty and then seemingly summoned to adventure, enchantment, and joy among friends. To the children's surprise, these columns of color could be moved, and they soon began to manipulate them. With each small movement, the impact was grand. The children giggled as they stretched and released the large coils, gleefully discovering their spring reaction. Immersed in the glowing corkscrews of plastic, the children and their research continued in this new direction, color enhancing the children's understanding of movement, and movement, in turn, enhancing their understanding of color. They also experimented with science and mathematical concepts such as reflection, shape, length, height, laws of motion, gravity, force, resistance, and cause and effect. Encompassed by the mirrors, the Slinkies, their motions, and the concepts with which the children grappled appeared to go on endlessly. We wondered how we might further make visible the traces of their research by leaving trails across the mirrored canvas.

For the next microenvironment installation, the children were fully immersed again in the cascading Slinkies, this time in a black box with paintbrushes dipped in neon paint and attached to the end of the coils. Fascination streamed across their faces as they intently studied the potentials of a Slinky with a paintbrush attached. Trails and traces of the children's inquiry were captured in paint as the motions of the children were mirrored by the motions of the coils and subsequent paintbrushes. As the children noticed the marks illuminating on the canvas beneath them, they began constructing and testing theories—altering both their motions and the chain reactions that followed. Each experimental attempt deepened their inquiry and built meaning regarding causality and chain reactions of motion as the children built an "alphabet of marks" to represent these phenomena.

Chapter 9 explores the power of iterative transformation, when teachers add or subtract intelligent and curated materials based on analysis of the children's interests and investigations. Seen through the evolution of a microenvironment within the color lab, focusing on the integration of black light, neon color, movement, and mark making, this chapter weaves children's strategies and interests with educator observations that inform the design of threaded, innovative experiences. The educators pose questions regarding the potential strategies, materials, provocations, and research opportunities within this space, aiming to deepen children's understanding of black light, neon color, and the mesmerizing altered perspective they afford.

Materials such as fluorescent circle streamers, painted bubble wrap, neon tape, brushes attached to Slinkies that dip into neon paint, and neon-patterned playground balls prompt experimentation with concepts such as circularity, gradient movement, cause and effect, mark making, transformation of color, and shifts in perspective, fostering a deeper understanding of scientific and mathematical principles.

Chapter 10: Long-Term Projects: Building Threads of Continuity

The two-year-old children were captivated by cicadas, small insects that emerge from the ground each summer. They watched in wonder as they observed the bugs climb onto a tree, shed their exoskeletons, and fly away. Daily, the children spent hours watching this process as they played on the playgrounds and throughout the woods. We observed the children recreating the "story of the cicada" in their play, in their drawings or paintings, and as they engaged in animated conversations with each other at the lunch table. Compelled by an opportunity to gather data and investigate, the children began documenting their findings through photography and creating their first portraits of cicadas.

We wondered what minute details the children would uncover with the use of a digital microscope, a small microscope that projects an image of a specimen that children place and manipulate under the lens onto a computer or through a projector. Studying the world through this lens brought to life the mysteries and surprises of scale. How might this micro vs. macro duality bring perspective to our inquiry? How could the use of a large-scale projection better our understanding of the details found on the cicada?

Simultaneously, a group of children began using acorns, twigs, small stones, miniature seashells, feathers, and sand to construct cicada wings in the dirt on the playground. Their attention to detail was profound. As we observed and photographed the children's spontaneous work, we began creating an informal inventory of possibilities for future experiences in robust environments full of relevant and intelligent materials. We wondered how we might build on the children's natural materials compositions. What other parts of the cicada intrigued the children?

How might they represent them?

Map of Thinking/Unfolding Concepts

- Cicada anatomy: eye, wings, body
- Nature
- Placement
- Projection
- Gathering
- Color
- Decomposition
- Composition
- Collaboration
- Communication
- Design

We began by projecting one of the images the children had captured through the digital microscope onto a low, white table. Using twigs of various sizes, the children outlined the wings' details. Each new day brought continued exploration of size, angle, space, shape,

and texture, and of the nuances of color as the children continued to add treasures to the wings. They competently navigated various tools, techniques, and strategies as they delicately placed tiny petals, seeds, and leaves. The unfolding work incited joy and wonder and supported the ongoing collaboration, problem solving, and perseverance toward a common goal.

Provocation 1

Provocation: Projection of cicada wing and design

Materials:

- Projector
- Gathered sticks
- Foam core
- White box studio
- Rocks

Questions:

How might we represent the cicada's wing through our collection of materials?

Reflection:

"We use a itty little glue." —Rex

"I place this one here I break it a little." —Russell

"We need flowers for it." —Addy

"I make the cicada wing." —Felix

"I connect it." —J. P.

The children worked in synchronous harmony as they collaborated and glued each stick.

Provocation 2

Provocation: (continued from previous provocation)

Materials: (continued from previous provocation)

Questions:

What additional layers might be added as we revisit the outline construction of the cicada wing?

Reflection:

"Oh, our cicada wing." —Jade

"Look, the black glue. It will stick. It is so sticky." —Anderson

"Look, look! What we made." —Graham

Time to pause and ask the children if more sticks are needed.

"I know. He needs two wings." —Callun, with one finger raised

Provocation 3

Provocation: Micro cicada-wing document, use to examine possible colors and deconstruction of flowers

Materials:

- Image of cicada wing by children with microscope
- Flower petals, various colors
- Scissors

Questions:

How might reflecting on and analyzing their cicada wing deepen the study and inspire creativity?

What additional layers might the children add to the cicada wing?

Reflection:

"It is our cicada wing. I see yellow." —Malcolm

"We need green and blue." —Jensen

"Purple. We need pink flowers. Mommy has pink flowers at home."

School-to-home connection: Ask parents to gather flowers with their children to bring to school.

Provocation 4

Provocation: Hues of yellow dried flowers, cicada wing

Materials:

- Cicada wing image
- Stick cicada wing artifact
- Dried yellow flowers
- Glue
- Tweezers

Questions:

How might the children begin to design the cicada wing with the various yellow hues?

Reflection:

"Flowers have to go inside the cicada wing." —Graham

"Some is green and some is not. Wow, this is going to look great." —Quincy

Collaboration, communication, and negotiation of space, placement, and agreements made among peers

Provocation 5

Provocation: Hues of blue added outdoors in nature, Honeysuckle Knoll

Materials:

- Woods walk
- Tweezers
- Glue
- Stick cicada wing

Questions:

How might bringing our cicada wing into the woods invite the beauty of nature to our work?

Reflection:

The children embraced the opportunity to design with the various shades of blue in nature.

New techniques with tweezers

New glue strategies

The children were remarkably proud of their work and announced that the wings needed a "whole cicada to go with it." We asked clarifying questions regarding their vision, and as we conversed it became clear that a three-dimensional bug sculpture was what they envisioned. They deemed their next task to be the body and the eyes. They were determined that the eyes be composed of beans and seeds and that the body had to be "full" and not flat. They were unsure, however, about what materials to use for the body. Again, we created an inventory of possibilities, wondering what materials and experiences could lend themselves to the children's goals. After brainstorming many ideas, we wondered whether textiles and chicken wire could provide a three-dimensional canvas for the body. We offered our ideas to the children, and they embraced the concept of a chicken-wire sculpture.

As a group, we began collecting materials and organizing them by color and texture in anticipation of beginning the next phase of the children's work. Once the children felt they had enough supplies, they began constructing the cicada body and eyes. They divided themselves into teams to accomplish their tasks. They shaped the wire form with help from the teachers, then they wired it closed, creating a tubelike structure. Small, competent hands wove ribbons and fabric of various textures and colors through the holes, creating a billowing puff for the body.

With magnified images of a cicada eye as a reference, the children working on this element began carefully analyzing the details of a cicada eye and placed beans and seed with precision to re-create the image. The effect was a whimsical representation that began to synthesize the various visions the children had for a sculpture.

Returning to their prior research and the beloved cicada image used throughout the process, the children noticed two important details: a cicada has four wings, and the wings have an iridescent nature. Originally, the children suggested clay as a medium for creating the needed wings, but after creating, glazing, and firing the first iteration, they were unimpressed by the lack of shimmer that glazed and fired clay provided. After regrouping and brainstorming, the children asked for a "materials hunt" to research possibilities.

The children found shelves full of iridescent beads and were thrilled to discover they were available for the taking. Gathering their found treasures, the two-year-olds returned to the classroom to decide what pallet would lend itself to the translucency necessary for their beads to sparkle. Remembering work they had done previously on an enclosed laser cutter, one child suggested we laser cut acrylic sheets in the shape of their sketched wings. The class was excited by the prospect and immediately reserved the laser cutter and formatted their document in preparation for cutting. They waited anxiously as their sketch transformed into an acrylic pallet and then organized themselves into groups to place the chosen beads. Their end result captured the luminescent qualities of a wing, and they were ecstatic at the outcome of their hard work.

With all of the individual pieces complete, the children were challenged to create what they called the "cicada puzzle." Returning to the original inspirational image, the children strategized ways to create a map that might support them. Ultimately, they decided to enlarge the image and lay the elements atop it. Next, the children began to piece together their puzzle. The result was astounding.

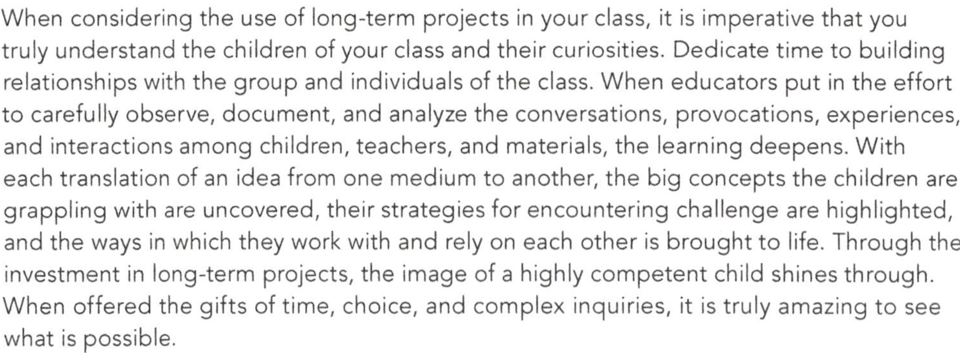

When considering the use of long-term projects in your class, it is imperative that you truly understand the children of your class and their curiosities. Dedicate time to building relationships with the group and individuals of the class. When educators put in the effort to carefully observe, document, and analyze the conversations, provocations, experiences, and interactions among children, teachers, and materials, the learning deepens. With each translation of an idea from one medium to another, the big concepts the children are grappling with are uncovered, their strategies for encountering challenge are highlighted, and the ways in which they work with and rely on each other is brought to life. Through the investment in long-term projects, the image of a highly competent child shines through. When offered the gifts of time, choice, and complex inquiries, it is truly amazing to see what is possible.

Appendix: Glossary

Action research: the cycle of inquiry inherent in the daily explorations and investigations of children and teachers

Atelier: a shared workspace where learners create

Big idea: overarching project

Cognitive dissonance: mental discomfort from holding two conflicting beliefs, values, or attitudes

Cognitive knot: a point of challenge that helps learning move forward

Concept: an abstract idea or general notion

Deep dive: digging deeper in multiple areas of a big idea to explore the parts

Disequilibrium: a state of uncertainty

Domains: areas of learning such as cognitive, affective, psychomotor

Game: child-invented play with others

Makerspace: a common space for collaboration, creativity, and innovation that offers tools, technology, and resources

Paradigm: a typical example or pattern of something; a model

Refraction: the bending of light or sound as it passes through something

Social construction: a concept that exists not in objective reality but as a result of human interaction

Thinking toes: the curling of toes when children are in deep concentration

Thinking tongue: the sticking out or movement of the tongue in concentration as children are exploring materials

Trickery: use of illusions to further questions

References and Recommended Reading

Bellanca, James A. 2015. *Deeper Learning: Beyond 21st Century Schools*. Bloomington, IN: Solution Tree Press.

Berger, Warren. 2014. *A More Beautiful Question: The Power of Inquiry to Spark Breakthrough Ideas*. New York: Bloomsbury.

Bruner, Jerome. 1979. *On Knowing: Essays for the Left Hand*. Cambridge, MA: Belknap Press.

Bruner, Jerome. 1990. *Acts of Meaning: Four Lectures on Mind and Culture*. Cambridge, MA: Belknap Press.

Cagliari, Paola, et al., eds. 2016. *Loris Malaguzzi and the Schools of Reggio Emilia: A Selection of His Writings and Speeches*, 1945–1993. London, UK: Routledge.

Ceppi, Giulio, and Michele Zini, eds. 1998. *Children, Spaces, Relations: Metaproject for an Environment for Young Children*. Reggio Emilia, IT: Reggio Children.

Couros, George. 2015. *The Innovator's Mindset: Empower Learning, Unleash Talent, and Lead a Culture of Creativity*. San Diego, CA: Dave Burgess Consulting, Inc.

Dewey, John. 1938. *Experience and Education*. New York: Macmillan.

Dweck, Carol. 2006. *Mindset: The New Psychology of Success*. New York: Random House.

Dweck, Carol. 2017. "The Impact of a Growth Mindset." Mindset Works. https://www.mindsetworks.com/science/Impact

Edwards, Carolyn, Lella Gandini, and George Forman, eds. 2011. *The Hundred Languages of Children: The Reggio Emilia Experience in Transformation*. 3rd ed. Westport, CT: Praeger.

Freire, Paulo. 2018. *Pedagogy of the Oppressed*. New York: Bloomsbury Academic.

Gandini, Lella, and Carolyn Edwards, eds. 2001. *Bambini: The Italian Approach to Infant/Toddler Care*. New York: Teachers College Press.

Gandini, Lella, Susan Etheredge, and Lynn Hill, eds. 2008. *Insights and Inspirations from Reggio Emilia: Stories of Teachers and Children from North America*. Worcester, MA: Davis.

Gandini, Lella, Lynn Hill, Louise Cadwell, and Charles Schwall, eds. 2005. *In the Spirit of the Studio: Learning from the Atelier of Reggio Emilia*. New York: Teachers College Press.

Giudici, Claudia, Carlina Rinaldi, and Mara Krechevsky, eds. 2001. *Making Learning Visible: Children as Individual and Group Learners*. Reggio Emilia, IT: Reggio Children and Harvard Project Zero.

Hawkins, David. 1974. *The Informed Vision: Essays on Learning and Human Nature*. New York: Agathon Press.

Hawkins, Frances P. 1969. *The Logic of Action: From a Teacher's Notebook*. New York: Pantheon Books.

Jacobs, Heidi H. 2010. *Curriculum 21: Essential Education for a Changing World*. Alexandria, VA: ASCD.

Malaguzzi, Loris, and Paola Cagliari. 2018. *Brick by Brick: History of the XXV Aprile People's Nursery School of Villa Cella*. Reggio Emilia, IT: Reggio Children.

Manet, Édouard. n.d. "Édouard Manet Quotes." https://www.manet.org/

Martinez, Sylvia L., and Gary Stager. 2013. *Invent to Learn: Making, Tinkering, and Engineering in the Classroom*. Torrence, CA: Constructing Modern Knowledge Press.

Municipality of Reggio Emilia. 2010. *Indications: Preschools and Infant-Toddler Centres of the Municipality of Reggio Emilia*. English ed. Reggio nell'Emilia, Emilia-Romagna, IT: Municipality of Reggio Emilia.

Pink, Daniel H. 2006. *A Whole New Mind: Why Right-Brainers Will Rule the Future*. New York: Riverhead Books.

Reggio Children. 2011. *The Wonder of Learning: The Hundred Languages of Children*. Reggio Emilia, IT: Reggio Children.

Reggio Children. 2015. *Mosaic of Marks, Words, Material*. Reggio Emilia, IT: Reggio Children.

Reggio Children. 2019. *Bordercrossings: Encounters with Living Things/Digital Landscapes*. Reggio Emilia, IT: Reggio Children.

Rinaldi, Carlina. 2003. "The Teacher as Researcher." *Innovations in Early Education: The International Reggio Exchange* 10(2).

Rinaldi, Carlina. 2004. "The Relationship Between Documentation and Assessment." *Innovations in Early Education: The International Reggio Exchange* 11(1). https://www.reggioalliance.org/downloads/relationship:rinaldi.pdf

Rinaldi, Carlina. 2006. *In Dialogue with Reggio Emilia: Listening, Researching and Learning*. London, UK: Routledge.

Ritchhart, Ron. 2015. *Creating Cultures of Thinking: The 8 Forces We Must Master to Truly Transform Our Schools*. San Francisco: Jossey-Bass, Wiley.

Robinson, Ken. 2010. "Changing Education Paradigms." TEDTalk. https://www.ted.com/talks/sir_ken_robinson_changing_education_paradigms

Sobel, David. 2024. "About David Sobel." David Sobel. https://www.davidsobelauthor.com/about-david-sobel

Tough, Paul. 2012. *How Children Succeed: Grit, Curiosity, and The Hidden Power of Character.* New York: HarperCollins.

Vecchi, Vea, ed. 2002. *Theater Curtain: The Ring of Transformation.* Reggio Emilia, IT: Reggio Children.

Vecchi, Vea. 2010. *Art and Creativity in Reggio Emilia: Exploring the Role and Potential of Ateliers in Early Childhood Education.* London, UK: Routledge.

Vecchi, Vea, and Claudia Giudici, eds. 2004. *Children, Art, Artists: The Expressive Languages of Children, the Artistic Language of Alberto Burri.* Reggio Emilia, IT: Reggio Children.

Wagner, Tony. 2008. *The Global Achievement Gap: Why Even Our Best Schools Don't Teach the New Survival Skills Our Children Need—and What We Can Do about It.* New York: Basic Books.

Wagner, Tony. 2012. Creating Innovators: *The Making of Young People Who Will Change the World.* New York: Scribner.

Wagner, Tony, and Ted Dintersmith. 2015. *Most Likely to Succeed: Preparing Our Kids for the Innovation Era.* New York: Scribner.

Index

S